SECOND EDITION

Creative Play Activities for Children With Disabilities

Human Kinetics Books

Champaign, Illinois

Library of Congress Cataloging-in-Publication Data

Morris, Lisa Rappaport, 1957-
   Creative play activities for children with disabilities : a
resource book for teachers and parents / Lisa Rappaport Morris,
Linda Schulz. -- 2nd ed.
      p.   cm.
   Rev. ed. of: Recipes for fun.
   Bibliography: p.
   ISBN 0-87322-933-9
   1. Handicapped Children--Recreation.   2. Creative activities
and seat work.   I. Schulz, Linda, 1941-   . II. Morris,
Lisa Rappaport, 1957-   . Recipes for fun.   III. Title.
GV183.6S38   1989
790.1'96--dc 19   88-8540
                                                            CIP

Developmental Editor: Lisa Busjahn; **Production Director:** Ernie Noa;
Copyeditor: Barbara Walsh; **Proofreader:** Karin Leszczynski; **Managing Editor:** Holly Gilly; **Typesetter:** Cindy Pritchard; **Text Design:** Keith Blomberg;
Text Layout: Jayne Clampitt; **Illustrations:** Ingrid Gehle; **Cover Design:** Jack
Davis; **Printed By:** United Graphics, Inc.

ISBN: 0-87322-933-9

Printed in the United States of America   20   19   18   17   16

Human Kinetics
Web site: www.humankinetics.com

United States: Human Kinetics, P.O. Box 5076, Champaign, IL 61825-5076
800-747-4457
e-mail: humank@hkusa.com

Canada: Human Kinetics, 475 Devonshire Road, Unit 100, Windsor, ON N8Y 2L5
800-465-7301 (in Canada only)
e-mail: orders@hkcanada.com

Europe: Human Kinetics, Units C2/C3 Wira Business Park, West Park Ring Road
Leeds LS16 6EB, United Kingdom
+44 (0) 113 278 1708
e-mail: hk@hkeurope.com

Australia: Human Kinetics, 57A Price Avenue, Lower Mitcham, South Australia 5062
08 8277 1555
e-mail: liahka@senet.com.au

New Zealand: Human Kinetics, P.O. Box 105-231, Auckland Central
09-523-3462
e-mail: hkp@ihug.co.nz

In memory of my father, George Rappaport, who taught me the importance of determination and perseverance in meeting all that life brings.

LRM

CONTENTS

Chapter 5—Exploring the World of Arts and Crafts . . 119

Chapter 6—Exploring the World of Music and Rhythm 145

Chapter 7—Exploring the World of Group Activities 171

The Joseph P. Kennedy, Jr. Foundation

1350 NEW YORK AVENUE, N.W., SUITE 500
WASHINGTON, D.C. 20005-4709
(202) 393-1250

Dear Readers:

I'm very pleased to announce the second edition of this activities resource book. *Creative Play Activities for Children With Disabilities* provides many new games and activities and a chapter with special tips that will help you make playtime with your children joyful.

The activities and games in this edition are an outgrowth of more than ten years of experience with children with disabilities and their families in the Let's Play to Grow Program developed by the Joseph P. Kennedy, Jr. Foundation.

Creative Play Activities for Children With Disabilities recognizes the determination of teachers and parents to wisely use the opportunities recently mandated by Congress to encourage the early development of children with disabilities. Research confirms that development can be enhanced if parents play naturally with their young children; are responsive to their interests, needs, and capabilities; and enjoy sharing the fun themselves.

This book provides the resources teachers and parents can use together to plan how to reinforce development goals and, perhaps most important, how to stimulate the sense of fun and enjoyment all families need for healthy growth.

Creative Play Activities for Children With Disabilities is for all the teachers and parents who provide the vision, planning, and courage necessary to work together with very special children.

With admiration and good wishes,

Eunice Kennedy Shriver

Eunice Kennedy Shriver
Executive Vice President
Joseph P. Kennedy, Jr. Foundation

PREFACE

Creative Play Activities for Children With Disabilities has been designed to promote the development of young children with disabilities through play and games—the kinds of learning activities which come most naturally to the young child. This second edition of the book, as did the first, focuses on the family as the center of the young child's play and learning environment. However, we believe that this expanded edition will have even wider use as educators and other professionals work with special families to meet the challenges of providing new opportunities for preschool children with disabilities, as recently directed by federal legislation on education. In addition to assisting parents to provide expanded play and learning opportunities at home, *Creative Play Activities for Children With Disabilities* also provides a wealth of ideas and resources for use in the classroom and in therapy sessions. Teachers, therapists, and parents together can have the greatest impact on helping children reach their developmental potentials.

The most important ingredients for these play activities are still those teachers, other professionals, and parents add themselves—sensitivity to the child's needs and interests and those of other family or group members, a willingness to enter into the spirit of fun, pride in a child's achievements, and personal creativity and warmth.

The book contains hundreds of activities, games, and directions for making simple homemade toys for children with mild to severe disabilities ranging in age from birth to 8. Each chapter focuses on a particular "world," or activity theme, such as sensory, motor, or water and outdoor play. Each activity lists detailed directions, and the items that will be needed, the activity's benefits, and, possible, adaptations for different disabilities.

Because no two children progress at the same rate, we did not include a developmental scale or reference to specific ages for each activity. Almost all groups and families consist of persons of varying ages, abilities, and interests. Teachers know their students and parents know their families better than anyone. We are confident all will choose the games and activities that will provide the most enjoyable play for each child.

Educators and family members may need to try various adaptations of an activity to help the child fully enjoy play. In this edition, Chapter 1, "Tips for Successful Playtimes," provides helpful suggestions that teachers and parents can use to create fun, positive play experiences. Also included are some general principles for adapting play for children who are blind or visually impaired, deaf or hearing impaired, and physically impaired. These guidelines should be kept in mind throughout the book's activities. They will provide ways to make playtime rewarding.

Each chapter progresses from simple games and activities to more difficult and developmentally advanced ones. Where several similar games are grouped together, the first games listed are simpler than the last games. The activities in chapters 2, 3, and 4 are appropriate for infants and toddlers. The activities in chapters 5, 6, and 7 are not. Yet, if you use your imagination you will find many ways to include the very young in activities with family, friends, and other group members. For example, you can place the child in the center of a circle game, make sure he or she is close enough to hear a family song fest, or physically guide his or her hands through an art activity. At the back of the book, are lists of associations, newsletters, magazines, books, and adaptive toys that can be used for information and ideas for future fun and continuing growth.

Believing that during the early years many benefits of play are similar whether an educator or a parent is guiding the child, we have decided to address the parents and focus on questions and concerns they have about interacting with their children. We believe this will encourage sharing between educators and parents and continuity between home and school and other program activities.

As you explore *Creative Play Activities for Children With Disabilities* you will meet the members of the Rainbow Bunch. These are five families who, like you, are facing the special challenges of having a young child with disabilities in the family. They are the Blues, the Greens, the Golds, the Violets, and the Reds. Throughout the book, they share with you the games they use both at home and when joining others at play.

It is very important to understand that although each Rainbow Bunch family is as unique and special in its needs and interests as your own, all of the games in this book are designed to be adapted for children with various disabilities. So when you are introduced to Leslie Blue in chapter 2, do not assume that because Leslie is 14 months old, has cerebral palsy, and is mildly retarded, the games described in chapter 2 will fit only a child with Leslie's characteristics.

Some chapters in this book use the pronoun *he* and others *she*. This is done not only to make activity directions match the gender of the child with disabilities whose family's activities are featured in that chapter, but also to emphasize the fact that all activities are for both boys and girls. Creating relaxed family play is one of the many challenges that confront families with disabled children. But the effort is indeed worthwhile. The bond created by sharing family fun can provide the energy, commitment, and strength needed to get through rough times the family will almost inevitably have to face.

Picture your family enjoying a kite party on a breezy March day. As you help to construct and decorate a brightly colored kite and watch it rise with the wind, everyone in the family, from the youngest toddler to Mom and Dad, will experience a sense of accomplishment, a feeling of closeness from participating in a successful team effort, and relaxed escape from the more serious pressures of life.

ACKNOWLEDGMENTS

We would like to acknowledge the following individuals who assisted in the preparation of *Creative Play Activities for Children With Disabilities* as members of a national advisory panel of parents and professionals. Their unique blend of keen editorial judgement, professional and personal experiences, and commitment to the spirit of this project was a key element in the development of this book. Our special thanks go to the following members of the advisory panel: Ruthlee F. Adler, R.M./B.C.; Mark L. Batshaw, M.D.; Helene Berk, M.Ed.; Deborah Booth; Marcia Coling, M.A.; Robert E. Cooke, M.D.; Lillian Davis; Cheryl Decker; Sarah deVincentis; Emma Domoszlai; Herbert J. Kramer, Ph.D.; Jeannette Langeman; Sister Geraldine O'Brien; Dianne Philibosian, Ph.D.; Michael J. Pickett, M.A., C.T.R.S.; Cordie Puttkammer, O.T.R.; Jessie Rasmussen; Carrie Rymash; Beulah Thomas; Josie Thomas; Julie Wiley; and George Zitnay.

Grateful acknowledgment is made to the following for permission to use the songs listed: "Colors," "Rhythm Stick Game," and "The Hat" from *Target on Music,* 1982, by Ruthlee Adler, Rockville, MD: Christ Church Child Center, now Glenbrook Day School; "Big Drum Beats" by Dorothy Scott in *Magic of Music, Book One,* 1965, by Corrain E. Watters, et al., New York: Ginn and Co., adapted by Susan Gurley and Kathyrn Racette; "Look at David," lyrics by Grace Cangialosi; "Hit It One," by Betty Foster, *Training Songs for Special People,* 1979, Colorado: Myklass Music Press, 1979, adapted by Gerri Davis.

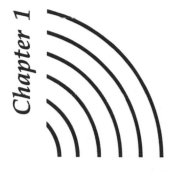

TIPS FOR SUCCESSFUL PLAYTIMES

As the parent of a child with disabilities, you may feel that little in your past experience has directly prepared you for the many challenges you are now facing. As you play with your child using the games and activities in *Creative Play Activities for Children With Disabilities* as well as those you create yourself, you will soon learn what kinds of play come easily and naturally. The experiences of others who have loved and cared for children with disabilities can be helpful, too. We've collected these tips from parents, teachers, therapists, and others who have worked with children with disabilities. We hope they will give you some good ideas for

- picking games and activities that are right for your child,
- adapting them to your child's needs, and
- organizing activities so that your child, as well as your whole family, gets into the act.

Most parents understand that for children in the early developmental stages almost every activity contains some element of play. What many parents may not realize is that "child's play" is the most important way children develop intellectually, socially, emotionally, and physically. Young children are natural explorers.

They are never still and seldom silent. They learn by trial and error as they play and experiment. A child with disabilities is no exception. Although physical or mental impairments may limit a child's ability to explore, the inner longing to explore the world remains.

For all children, play has several important and universal characteristics. The first is self-motivation. In other words, even if your child needs some specific help and guidance to gain the most from early experiences, play will spring from your child's own interests and developmental needs. Second, play is joyous and pleasurable. Though we adults can understand and promote the important role of play in development, for the child play is an end in itself, to be enjoyed for its own sake. The goal of play is to have fun, to enjoy others, to experiment and make mistakes, and to practice skills in a natural way.

Play for Fun and Learning

Although your child may have difficulties moving, coordinating eyes with hands, understanding or using language, or perceiving himself or herself and the world with one sense or another, you can ensure that your child will experience the pleasures and developmental gains that come from being able to play naturally. The special techniques described in this chapter will help you enrich your child's world and adapt activities so that play can become a natural, relaxed part of your family life. These techniques are not therapeutic remedies designed, or able, to solve all your child's developmental problems.

Parents sometimes feel that their job is not just to play with their child but rather to try to structure every part of the daily routine to compensate for the child's physical or mental impairments. This attitude may turn playtime into a training session. Parents may also assume that only expertly designed activities will promote their disabled child's development. This approach can place a heavy burden on all family members and undermine parents' confidence in their own parenting abilities. It may also make mothers and fathers ignore the spontaneous, simple, or traditional activities that should be an integral part of family play for every child. In addition, sometimes children are so absorbed in their play that to have an adult enter their world and change the course of their activity takes away from its fun and spontaneity. There are times when children can and should initiate their own play activities. This helps them develop a sense of competency and is a very important part of the learning process.

To help your child get the most benefit from play, you must understand some of the ways in which play develops. In the earliest developmental stages, a child discovers his or her body through play and exploring, by getting to know the face, hands, feet, and other parts of the body. The child tests and develops muscle control, vocal cords, and senses. Through playful, loving interaction with family members and others, children begin to understand the social world in which they live and to feel that they are loved and valued members of it. Through handling, tasting, smelling, and seeing toys and other objects, children gain an understanding of how the physical world works.

Young children also go through changes in social behavior. In the early stages of play, children enjoy smiles, caresses, songs, and conversations but have a difficult time focusing attention on more than one person at a time. At the next stage, children like to play near other children and adults, but show little interest in activities that require cooperation. For example, a child at this stage enjoys sitting with another child in a sandbox, but not actively playing with the other child.

Finally, in the later stages of play, children begin to take pleasure in games that require sharing, group cooperation, and taking turns with others, as well as make-believe and role playing. For example, children's sandbox play at this stage could include such activities as working together to build a network of roads for their toy cars or sharing a sandy pretend tea party.

Play for Family Unity

Your child's first learning experiences occur at home. This is where your child discovers the world and forms initial bonds of attachment to other human beings through interaction with parents and siblings. Perhaps the most important family interaction is play, for family play promotes the child's development as a social being and a sense of joy in living. Both dad and mom bring an added dimension to family playtimes by giving the gift of their creativity and experiences in childhood play activities.

Brothers and sisters have an important role, too. They form a child's first and possibly most influential relationship with others close in age. Brothers and sisters are role models for each other. They are available as long-term playmates and companions to provide emotional support. Because the disabled child's contacts with nondisabled children may be limited, relationships with brothers and sisters take on added importance. Play is one of the most important ways for a child with disabilities and his siblings to interact in a positive way.

Parents may be surprised at first to find that their children don't always play together happily or enjoy each other's company. Experienced parents know that a certain amount of fighting, jealousy, and other problems between brothers and sisters is natural in any family. One of the most common reasons for this friction is competition for their parents' attention. This sibling rivalry can be intensified when there is a disabled child in the family because of the extra time, care, and attention given the disabled child. Your other children may need a little help to understand some of the special techniques required to compensate for your disabled child's mental or physical impairment. This and other challenges will be discussed in the following sections.

Begin by Getting to Know Your Child

Think about what you have observed about your child's reactions. What is your child like when happy, interested, or excited? Bored, tired, hungry, or frustrated? Can your child focus on one activity for a long time, or is he easily distracted? Does your child avoid new experiences, or seek them out? What activities does your child do alone? When does your child need help?

What you find out by these kinds of observations can help you make the most of playtime. For example, if a child seems frustrated or agitated by a particular activity, that child may be saying that it is too difficult. If the child seems overstimulated, distracted, and unable to focus, this may be a signal that the child cannot block out many of the sights and sounds of the environment to focus on the immediate activity. By watching carefully to see how your child reacts in various situations, you will learn to read your child's messages, enabling you to discover abilities, likes, and dislikes.

Respond to your child's messages, whether physical or verbal. Don't assume that there is one formula that is right for every child or every situation. Responding sensitively and flexibly to your child's needs is a basic ingredient of a helping, caring relationship. It will demonstrate to your child that you see him as a unique and valued person. For example, if your child is fearful of new experiences or easily overstimulated, provide a quiet atmosphere and slowly present one activity at a time—such as cuddling, rocking, or a quiet game like Rub My Back (see chapter 2). This will show your child that you can be trusted to set comfortable limits. Eventually your child will feel more adventurous about trying more exciting activities.

Set the Scene for Fun and Learning

The environment in which your child plays can be very important. Some things to think about when planning your child's play are:

- Time. Keep play periods short. End them before your child gets bored or tired. Two or three short periods of play per day are often better than one long one.
- Comfort. Find the place where your child will be most comfortable and relaxed. For example, sitting on the floor may be more fun than sitting at a table.
- Distractions. Sitting facing a plain wall may be better than sitting in the middle of the room. Eliminate all nonessential distractions from the play area.
- Noise. Carry out play activities in a room that is as quiet as possible.
- Lighting. A room with soft lighting or with just a spotlight on the play area sometimes helps the child to focus better.

You can do much to set the scene for happy and successful playtime activities.

Learn to Play With Your Child

While every child has a natural predisposition to play, just providing time to play is not enough. Children learn most play behavior by watching, playing with, and even being guided by others. This is especially true of your disabled child who will probably need even more help than most children to get the most out of play. Join in play with your child. Sit on the floor at your child's level during playtime. During an art session, paint your own masterpiece. If you are trying to teach your child to jump, you jump too.

Do not introduce too many games or activities at once. It is easier for the very young or severely disabled child to concentrate on one activity at a time. Besides, young children often love to repeat old, familiar games.

Your child also needs time to play alone and to do things independently. Give your child time to explore the different ways to use a toy, to create a picture, to roll a ball, to play with the box a toy came in rather than the toy itself. Choose toys that can be used for more than one kind of activity. Allow your child to make choices during playtime—a red ball or a yellow one, playing in the sandbox or building with blocks, a walk in the park or a backyard picnic.

If your child has difficulty understanding verbal instructions, demonstrate or physically guide him through an activity. Keep your verbal instructions simple, and use the same key words or actions each time you do a particular activity with your child. Get your child's attention by saying, "Tommy, look," or "Mary, listen." Expand play vocabulary by using simple words and sentences to describe what you are seeing and doing together.

When your child is not enjoying an activity because it is too difficult, you can break it down into smaller steps and guide him or her through one step at a time. Try the activity yourself before you start. Be sure you present each step in order. For example, to reach for and grab an object, a child must see the object, move his arm and hand toward it, open his hand, and then grasp the object. The first step in helping your child develop this ability is to help your child focus attention on the object. You can use a brightly colored object or one that makes an interesting noise. (In chapter 2 you will find many ideas for making games out of this kind of activity.)

Help Brothers and Sisters Join in Play

By carefully choosing appropriate play activities and giving lots of praise, attention, and guidance, you can do a great deal to ensure that your children enjoy playing together. Here are some things you can try.

- Establish reasonable, realistic expectations. Very young children may not interact with each other at all. Once your children have developed cooperative play skills, don't expect them to play together all the time or for long periods. Children of preschool age may be able to play together for only 10 or 12 minutes at most. Remember that playing with a disabled child can be a challenge, especially if the child has a severe disability or is not very active.

- Select activities and toys that encourage children to play together. For example, blocks, balls, and cars promote more social interaction than puzzles, stuffed animals, and paints.
- Use lots of praise when children play together well. Try to be specific in your praise. "Good girl! You're sharing your toys!" is much more effective than, "That's good."
- Directly promote cooperative play by guiding and modeling cooperative play yourself. For example, you can be one of the guests at a pretend tea party, a puppeteer in a puppet show, or one of the players in a game of tag. This book offers numerous suggestions for group games that you and your children can play together.
- Accentuate the positive. Praise and encouragement will help your children feel successful, appreciated, and motivated to keep on trying. A smile, a big hug, enthusiastic words, a sticker, or a favorite snack will reward them for trying, looking, and listening. Praise your children not only for even the smallest success, but also for just participating.
- Keep things fun and light. Show your own enthusiasm for the activity by your actions and tone of voice.
- Don't be frustrated if your children's efforts fail at first. As long as they are having fun, encourage them to continue trying. If a toy or game is too difficult for one of your children to play with, store it away for a few months, then try it again. In fact, you'll get more use out of toys if you periodically rotate them. What seemed old hat two months ago may seem exciting today.
- Begin playtime with an activity you know your child can do. Use success with this activity to encourage him to go on to new or more difficult activities.

These tips should help your whole family enjoy play activities.

Try to Support Your Child's Independence

Don't worry if your child wants to do something different from what you have in mind. The child may be testing limits or signaling that the activity you have chosen is either too difficult or too easy. Other reasons may include a desire to stick with a familiar routine or favorite game, or a stronger interest in another activity. For example, you begin to play ball with your child. You try every strategy you can think of to make the game attractive, but your child hides under the table. It is important to encourage this move toward independence. Try playing ball under the table, or put the ball away and make a game of hiding under the table.

While it's important to allow your child the freedom to initiate activities and develop a sense of independence, it is also important to set reasonable and consistent limits. Your young child needs to learn the boundaries of acceptable and safe behavior. Providing limits gives children a sense of security and a framework within which individualism and independence can flourish. Whenever possible, tell your child what he can do, rather than focusing on what he cannot. If your child wants to play in the toilet, say "no," and show him how to play with water in the sink, bathtub, or sprinkler.

Adapt Play to Your Child's Special Needs

Not all the activities in this book will work with every disabled child. Some will have to be adapted to meet the needs of specific disabling conditions. Some children may not be able to participate in certain activities at all. For example, in order to take part in activities that require large muscle movement, like the games found in chapter 4, a child must be able to control his own movement to some extent. However, most activities and games can be adapted so your child experiences the play necessary for growth and development. Use the adaptations for the games and activities in *Creative Play Activities for Children With Disabilities*, and use your imagination, ingenuity, and knowledge of your child to create your own adaptations. Here are some principles to keep in mind as you and your family enjoy playing together.

If Your Child Is Deaf or Hearing Impaired

The world of most young children is filled with sound—Mom cooing and chatting to her infant as she gives him a bath, Dad singing a lullaby at bedtime, a door slamming, the family dog barking, older sister asking for a cookie, big brother's radio blaring. As the hearing child grows and learns, environmental sounds and especially language tie the child's experiences together for a better understanding of the world.

You can make sure that your child who is deaf or hearing impaired has experiences that compensate for the inability to hear some or all sounds. When planning your child's daily routine and play activities, think about ways to help develop language and communication skills.

If your child wears a hearing aid, monitor the equipment to make sure it is in good working condition, free of dirt, wax, and breaks in the cord. The hearing aid should be checked periodically by an audiologist. The hearing aid amplifies all sounds. The child with a hearing aid has difficulty filtering out background noise from meaningful sounds and conversation. Give careful consideration to this problem by eliminating as much background noise as possible and selecting appropriate settings for play.

During play use visual and physical cues along with what you say. Physical communication is an important part of play during your child's earliest years. Social meanings of words can be conveyed to young children through interesting, warm, and loving facial expressions, pats, hugs, and kisses. Touch, and help your child touch and explore, objects and toys as you talk about them.

Be sure you and other family members have your child's attention before speaking. It is important to be at your child's eye level so he can see your face when you speak. Always speak naturally at normal volume and speed, but slow down and articulate words if you are normally a fast talker. Exaggerated lip movements may be confusing. Describe objects, events, and relationships during play and other daily routines. Encourage your child to communicate about his surroundings and experiences. Use open-ended questions such as, "Tell me about what you are making."

Encourage your child to communicate with you and other members of the family. Gestures used by a very young child who is deaf or hearing impaired serve the same functions as baby talk. If your baby or young child is using gestures, think of these as words and reinforce the intention behind the action. The first nonverbal communication skills your child develops will probably be expressions of pleasure and displeasure. Be sensitive to these signs; reinforce your child's efforts to communicate by responding appropriately.

During play periods as well as during other activities, allow your child adequate opportunity to respond. She might need extra time to formulate responses, whether in sign language, spoken English, or both. Determine what your child is expressing from the context of the particular situation. If you can understand an occasional word, repeat that word as a question.

Help your child to compensate for loss of hearing by making the most out of the senses of sight and touch. If your child is profoundly deaf, seeing and looking will be the most important ways your child will play, learn, and grow. Remove barriers to visual stimulation, and provide lots of visual experiences during play and other daily activities. Use games such as Touch Mobiles, Hide 'n' Find, and Flashlight Games, which can all be found in chapter 2.

Give your child the opportunity to explore rattles, mobiles, and soft toys. Vibrations and other sensations felt through touching and holding toys and other objects are important, since the child may not hear the sound the toy makes. Feeling moving parts in a rattle or a manipulative toy will also help your child develop a sense that he can make something happen and has control over his environment.

Introduce your child at an early age to play and social experiences with brothers and sisters as well as with other children. Provide the support and guidance he needs to play next to, and eventually with, others. Remember that shorter, more frequent play periods can be much more productive than longer ones, which often end in fatigue and frustration.

A hearing child picks up happenings and events in the home largely because they are tied together with language. It is mainly through language that children learn about consistency in day-to-day life. Be as consistent as possible with daily routines and set-ting and maintaining rules. It is also very important for all family members to learn to communicate with your child. During play, family activities, and daily routines, all family members should use your child's mode of communication. Early language experiences and free-flowing communication will enable your child to be an important and active part of the family.

If Your Child Is Blind or Visually Impaired

Children's earliest learning begins with the senses. If your child is visually impaired or blind, you can enhance his environment by structuring play activities that encourage exploring and learning about the world through touching, listening, tasting, and smelling. Again, language development is of utmost importance. Through associating words with sounds, smells, textures, and movement your child builds the foundation for later language and intellectual development.

Talk to your child about what you are doing even if you are just washing the dishes or making a bed. Describe the things around you both, what is happening, and what is going to happen next. Avoid using vague words, especially words associated with visual space, such as, "The toy is over there," or "The doll is in the middle of the room." Instead, use a familiar point of reference, such as, "The ball is under the table."

When you talk to your child, use the words, "look" and "see" to help him learn about an object or toy. It may seem awkward to ask a child who is visually impaired to look at something, but it is important to encourage your child to use whatever degree of residual vision is available to him. If your child is blind, his method of examining an object is by touching, feeling, listening, even tasting and smelling. If family members and friends begin to use the words "look" and "see" from the beginning, your child will come to understand what those words mean.

Describe and talk about the colors, lights, shapes, and sizes of the objects in your child's world. Light, color, and shape are especially useful in helping your child understand the surrounding space and environment. If your child has some degree of vision, make an extra effort to point out these things. Remember that it is natural for many children with partial vision to see better on some days than on others.

Help your child listen to, recognize, and identify voices and sounds by using activities such as Moving Sounds, Talking Sounds, Shake, Rattle, 'n' Roll, and All Kinds of Sounds games, which can be found in chapter 2. Be sure to talk about new sounds, particularly those that might be frightening, like an ambulance siren or a fire drill horn.

Praise and encourage your child when he makes the slightest pause, hesitation, or movement in response to sound. Encourage listening to the sounds. Promote your child's motivation to reach for, crawl, or move toward toys. Use sound cues such as your voice or musical toys to help orient your child during play. Surround your child with a variety of objects and toys with interesting textures, sounds, and odors. Use balls, rattles, and musical toys in the games you play. Toys that make noise and provide sound cues when properly connected are excellent for your child, as are toys that fit together, such as nesting cups, stacking rings, puzzles, and snap-together blocks. You can adapt many of the activities in *Creative Play Activities for Children With Disabilities* by using brightly colored, shiny, textured, or noise-making objects and toys. Through the senses of touching and hearing, your child will master the skills needed for fun and joy-filled play.

During play, place toys at or above your child's chest level to encourage good posture. Children who are blind or visually impaired may develop rounded backs because they tend to play with toys on the floor and do not hold their heads up to look at their surroundings. The posture that your child develops early in life has a great effect on the quality of his posture in adulthood.

During playtime help your child learn that a toy or object exists even when out of reach or out of sight. Encourage your child to search for and find a dropped or lost toy by sound and physically directing his arms in the direction of the toy.

Introduce your child to a new environment by using a familiar and obvious point of reference in the room, such as a door or large piece of furniture. Describe major features and objects as you move together around the room. Relate major features of the room back to the reference point. Repeat, moving around the room several times, always encouraging more independence. It is important to keep room arrangements constant and predictable to promote your child's safety and confidence.

Broadening your child's familiarity with his or her world, which encompasses various rooms and furniture, household objects, and the outdoors, where your child, his or her brothers, sisters, and friends may play, is very important. This is especially true for a child who is blind or visually impaired; otherwise understanding the world may become limited to his body parts and toys or objects that are handled often. It is common for a child with a visual impairment to be afraid of unfamiliar places, so observe your child's response to new situations and settings.

When your child is around sighted children, help him to explore what others are doing and to play in a way that is natural and fun. Your child needs to learn to play next to, and eventually with, other children. At first this can be frightening, so begin by helping your child to play with familiar people. Include him in activities with brothers and sisters, even if only for short periods of time. Remember, shorter play periods are usually more fun and successful for your child.

To learn and grow, your child needs to understand what he hears, touches, sees, and smells. With each new experience, give your child as much support as needed so he will feel a part of the family and the world. If you provide your child with the support and encouragement he needs, each new experience will bring with it an adventure of learning, growing, and sharing.

If Your Child Is Physically Impaired

Explore various situations and identify the special ingredients necessary to ensure positive, fun-filled play. Discuss your child's needs with a physical and/or occupational therapist. Questions to ask yourself and the therapist include:

- What positions will allow maximum freedom of movement while providing appropriate support?
- What is the best way to help my child get from one position to another?
- What materials or modifications of toys and other equipment are needed?
- What, if any, adaptive equipment is needed to help my child participate and enjoy play and other activities?
- What play activities will promote the kinds of movement that my child should practice?

In general, when playing with your child, position him or help him move into a position that will allow maximum range of motion, muscle control, and good visual contact with what he is doing. This can mean lying in a prone position over a bolster, sitting in a specially designed chair, or lying on his side or on an inclined surface. Never force a position. Proper positioning will also help prevent poor movement patterns from being established.

It is important to place the very young child in many different positions during play. This will enable him to see all the different kinds of activity that take place at home. When selecting an area at home for play, remove as many of the physical and environmental barriers that may interfere with your child's direct involvement with the activity as possible.

Children with physical impairments may have speech problems. If your child has feeding problems, that may be an early indication of later difficulties in speech and articulation. Work closely with your child's speech and language therapist to identify the types of play and other activities and supports your child may need to develop speech and language.

Give your child a variety of play opportunities to use small muscles and feel different textures and sensations. Activities in *Creative Play Activities for Children With Disabilities* such as Shaving Cream Masterpieces, Texture Box, Water Play, Sand Play, and Squeezy Weezy can provide your child with these experiences. For added fun, help your child to explore with his feet. Try making a footprint in play dough or painting with feet instead of fingers.

If your child can use both arms and hands, encourage the use of two hands at the same time. Shaving Cream Masterpieces and Pudding Paint are fun ways to use both hands. Involve your child in play activities that encourage him to move arms and legs across the center of his body. Rhythm Stick Game, Hit It One, Beanbag Toss, and Fishing in *Creative Play Activities for Children With Disabilities* will help promote this action.

If your child has the use of only one hand or has weak, uncoordinated hands, be sure to provide the physical assistance needed or the adaptive materials necessary to enable full participation in play activities. For example, if your child has minimal hand and grasp movement, attach one piece of Velcro to a mitten and another to a toy such as a block or small stuffed animal. Your child, wearing the mitten, can then pick up the object. Easy-to-manipulate switches and devices on battery-operated toys are also helpful.

If your child is not ambulatory and is unable to use his hands, many activities can be adapted for use with feet only. Examples include painting with the feet, using feet to build with blocks, wearing puppets on the feet, and placing bells on feet and legs during music activities. There are many things your child can do even without the use of body extremities. Crayons or paintbrushes can be attached to a headband. Your whole family can have fun with a blowing contest using feathers, balloons, or cotton balls. There are switches for battery-operated toys that your child can control with the head. Again, work closely with your physical and/or occupational therapist to create ways for your child to enjoy play and explore the environment.

In growing older, a child may begin to realize that an impairment limits full participation in play activities with brothers, sisters, and others. Provide as many opportunities as possible for your child to enjoy play activities with family and friends. Direct your child's attention to what he *can* do. Use appropriate techniques to adapt your child's environment or activities; give encouragement and emotional support. You can provide many of the same everyday experiences your child would get if he were able to move about freely.

Remember You're Not Alone

Parents of children with disabilities report that one of the most difficult emotions they face is the feeling that they are alone in having to cope with their child's disability. It is important for parents to reach out for help and support. In most communities, agencies and experts such as early childhood educators, counselors, speech and language pathologists, and occupational and physical therapists offer assistance to parents of children with disabilities. They can advise you on the best ways to promote your child's development, from selecting appropriate toys to dealing with behavior problems. There are also excellent books, magazines, and other materials to supplement the activities in *Creative Play Activities for Children With Disabilities* with ideas for teaching and playing with your child. See the resources lists at the end of the book or look for them in your local library.

Don't be afraid to reach out to relatives and friends. Other parents of children with disabilities can be particularly helpful in providing support and understanding. Join a parent support group, or form your own club where all members of your family can join together to share friendship, support, and fun with others who are going through similar experiences.

As your child grows older, you may find that the local YMCA, recreation department, school, Special Olympics, and other agencies offer play, recreation, and sports programs designed for children with disabilities and staffed by specially trained professionals or volunteers. Also, as your child's play progresses, it will become easier to include him or her in your community's mainstream recreational programs.

Use the activities in the next six chapters as a special way to help your family. Keep in mind the "Tips for Successful Playtimes" as you explore and experiment together. Throughout the activities, remember to respond sensitively to your child, guide and help him to learn, and above all else have fun...the rest will come naturally!

Chapter 2

EXPLORING THE
WORLD
OF THE SENSES

Joyous and meaningful first experiences come in a variety of colors, sounds, and textures. Sometimes they are so good you can almost taste them. They're all here for your family to discover through Touch 'n' Tell, Hear 'n' See games. This chapter includes a series of activities to help your special child learn about herself and the world through the senses of touch, sight, hearing, taste, and smell, as well as through physical activities using the magic of play.

Children are natural explorers. Curiosity motivates them to explore a constant array of new experiences that give them the foundation for growth and learning. For some children with disabilities, however, physical or mental impairments may hinder their ability to approach new experiences. Some children with disabilities seem content to sit and do nothing. Others seem so overstimulated by their environments that they cannot organize their experiences into meaningful learning. While physical and mental impairments may limit your child's ability to explore, the inner longing to discover the world still remains. Use these activities and other familiar games, including ones that you create yourself, to help your special child explore the world of the senses.

Use everyday activities, from cooking dinner to dressing, to provide opportunities for sensory play. Bathtime, for example, can

become a great Touch 'n' Tell game. As you touch or rub the different parts of your child's body, tell her what they are. Make it a game, saying, "I'm gonna get your foot!" Then slowly grab her foot. "I'm coming for your knee!" Then touch her knee. This is an easy and fun way for your child to learn the parts of the body and develop a sense of timing as she anticipates how the game will continue.

Since earliest learning experiences occur mainly through sensory stimulation, these games are designed for children who are still learning about themselves and exploring the environment with their senses. Many of the activities will also be fun and beneficial for children of all ages and ability levels, as well as their brothers and sisters.

The very young or severely disabled child may be able to pay attention to only one person at a time. Nevertheless, these activities encourage all family members to participate and take turns playing with your child. Encourage each family member to develop games that your child enjoys.

The Blue Family Plays Touch 'n' Tell, Hear 'n' See Games

The Blue Family will guide you through Touch 'n' Tell, Hear 'n' See. Leslie Blue is 14 months old. She is an active, happy child who is mildly retarded and has cerebral palsy. Leslie lives with her mother in the city. Because the motor part of Leslie's brain is not working properly, she has difficulty controlling her muscles and movements. Sometimes she loses her balance; she needs to be propped in certain positions to throw a ball or drop blocks into a bucket. None of these impairments has dampened Leslie's enthusiasm for play. By helping each other, Leslie and her mother play Touch 'n' Tell games all day long. Here are some of the games Leslie and her mother have played.

"Bathtime, Leslie," Mrs. Blue says. Leslie smiles. She knows what that means . . .

Rub-a-Dub-Dub Games

These games will help awaken your child's senses, improve self-awareness, and teach her about the parts of her body. These are the ingredients you'll need for this set of activities:

- ☆ Soft, snuggly blanket
- ☆ Cornstarch/baby powder*
- ☆ Large ball or bolster
- ☆ Very soft brush
- ☆ Spray bottle
- ☆ Water
- ☆ Towels of different textures
- ☆ Lotion or massage oil
- ☆ Basin, pot, or tub

---

*SAFETY NOTE

Cornstarch is a good nonallergenic substitute for baby powder.

Some children may find Rub-a-Dub-Dub activities extremely uncomfortable and react negatively. Often these children do not like to be held or cuddled; cry when placed on grass, sand, or other textures; fuss or pull away from touch; and refuse certain textures of food, clothing, and toys. You have probably heard professionals use terms like "sensory integration problems," "tactually defensive," or "hypersensitive to touch" to describe your child's reaction to touch. Your child is not rejecting you. Her brain interprets the feel of things differently. These children have a great need for tactile experiences. If your child shows a negative reaction to the feel of different textures or to being touched, try the following:

- An infant who is tactually defensive will usually tolerate firm, medium-level pressure. If the child is particularly defensive to being touched on the hands and feet, begin touching at the shoulders and move toward the hands. Then begin touching at the hips and move toward the feet.
- Use a firmer, brisker touch, particularly if your child is "floppy" or has decreased muscle tone.
- If your child has increased muscle tone, or is stiff and rigid, always introduce movement activities slowly and gently. Avoid sudden, quick movements.
- Let the child's hand do the rubbing while you direct the movement.
- Gradually introduce different tactile experiences for brief periods of time.
- Observe the child's reaction; learn what the child finds pleasurable.
- Consult with an occupational or physical therapist for ideas, activities, and more information.

Here are a few Rub-a-Dub-Dub games you can play with your child.

Rub-a-Dub-Dub Game

Wrap your child in a warm, snuggly blanket. If she is uncomfortable with the blanket, leave it off. Uncover her left arm and apply body lotion. Massage her arm lightly in a circular motion. As you do so, say, "This is lotion. I'm rubbing lotion on your arm." Next, apply powder in a circular motion with both hands. "See, I'm rubbing powder on your arm." Place her left arm back in the blanket and follow the same procedure with other parts of her body—legs, tummy, hands, feet, etc.—talking to her all the while. When she is able, let her identify her own body parts. To teach her about different degrees of pressure, rub her arm gently and tell her that you're rubbing her "gently." For extra fun, Mrs. Blue plays Pat-a-Cake on different parts of Leslie's body.

Hot Dog Game

Play this game without the blanket. Pretend your child is a hot dog or another favorite food. Apply "catsup" (lotion), "mustard" (cream), and "relish" (powder). Repeat the food game with a soft baby brush. Brush your child's arms and legs. Allow your child to control the activity by brushing her own arms and legs. Let her put lotion and powder on you and brush your arms.

Rub 'n' Dry Game

Using a spray bottle, spray water on your child's arms, legs, tummy, feet, back, and forehead, and help her rub dry with towels of varying textures. Help your child name the body parts being dried. Let your child dangle her feet in a tub of water, encouraging her to kick and move her feet.

Dough Roll Game

Firmly roll a ball or bolster up and down her body while she is wrapped in the blanket. She will find this to be very relaxing and soothing.

Tickle and Blow Game

Kiss your child's nose, ears, and fingers. Tickle and blow on other body parts. Always name the body parts you are touching. Make sure brother, sister, and Dad play this game too!

Adaptation for the Hearing Impaired. Attract your child's visual attention with your hands so your child understands that your movements communicate specific thoughts, ideas, and words. Use signs or gestures as you talk.

How to Make Mobiles and Mobile Fun

Mobiles will help your child use her eyes, ears, and body together. These are the ingredients you will need to make mobiles:

- ☆ Dowel
- ☆ Elastic
- ☆ Bells
- ☆ Vegetable brush
- ☆ String
- ☆ Squeak toys
- ☆ Pot holders
- ☆ Wooden thread spools

Here are ways to make and play with your mobiles.

Touch Mobiles

Secure a dowel to the legs of a table or the rung of a chair or crib. Tie two objects with different textures, such as a vegetable brush and a pot holder, to the dowel with the elastic. The objects must be small enough to be held but too large to be swallowed. Place the child on the floor or in the crib in a position that allows her to use her hands to play with the mobile. Some positions to try are lying on her back with the mobile over her chest, lying on her side with the mobile in front of her chest, lying on her tummy with the mobile in front of her, or sitting with the mobile in front of her. Laugh or smile as you bring the objects to touch your child's hand. Or let them hang and encourage her to reach for them. Mrs. Blue likes to add new objects every few days to give Leslie different tactile experiences. This game will help your child to explore the feel of soft, smooth, rough, and hard textures.

Sound Mobiles

Tie wooden spools and bells to a string. Be sure to fasten the items securely. Then anchor them to the mobile to add sound. Take your child's hand or foot and show her how she can gently tap on the mobile to produce sounds.

Brother/Sister Mobiles

Place a long, bright scarf around a brother's or sister's arm or wrist and have him/her move just above the child's chest, close enough for your child to reach and grab for the scarf. Hold rattles, squeaky toys, or other favorite objects in front of or to the side of your child. Encourage her to find the toy with her eyes and reach for it with her hand. Since Leslie doesn't have a brother or sister, Mrs. Blue sometimes invites Leslie's cousins to play this game with her.

```
┌─────────────────────────────────────────────────────────┐
│                      SAFETY NOTE                          │
│   Always supervise your child during these games to       │
│   prevent her becoming tangled in the strings or pulling  │
│   objects off the mobile.                                 │
└─────────────────────────────────────────────────────────┘
```

Adaptation for the Hearing Impaired.   Use brightly colored objects that will vibrate when held and moved.

Adaptation for the Visually Impaired.   Use shiny, bright-colored toys and objects and sound-making toys.

Adaptation for the Physically Impaired.   Use a sideways or supported sitting position, and gently push the child's shoulder or arms forward to reach the objects.

Stretch 'n' Reach Games

Try these activities to help your child reach for, grasp, and use tools to get her favorite toy. These are the ingredients you'll need for this set of activities:

☆ Mirror

☆ Favorite toys

☆ Small blanket

☆ String and thread spool

☆ Elastic

   Here are a few Stretch 'n' Reach games you can play with your child.

Where Are You? Game

Mrs. Blue sits in front of the mirror with Leslie on her lap and some favorite toys by their side. She points to Leslie in the mirror and says, "I see Leslie." She asks her to find Leslie. When Leslie looks and finds herself, Mrs. Blue gives her a big hug and smile. Then Mrs. Blue selects a teddy bear. She holds it just above Leslie's head and well within her reach. She asks her, "Where is Teddy?" and encourages her to reach for and hold Teddy. She tries this a few more times with different toys.

Pull and Play Game

Place your child in a propped or sitting position on your lap. Mom, Dad, or a brother or sister dangles a favorite toy tied to a nylon or elastic loop. Encourage your child to reach for and grasp her toy. After she has pulled it, give her time to play with it, and then start again. She will enjoy this give-and-take game more if the other players spice it up with lots of smiles. Use action words with this game, like "pull" and "let go."

Give and Take Game

Mrs. Blue places Leslie in a sitting position with a small blanket in front of her. She sits on the other side of the blanket and places a favorite toy on the blanket. Mrs. Blue pulls the blanket and reaches for and/or holds the toy. She places the toy back on the blanket and places the blanket within Leslie's reach. Now it is Leslie's turn to pull the blanket and take her toy. Use action words to describe what is happening.

Pull Toy Game

Mrs. Blue positions Leslie in a sitting position on her lap with a table top or flat surface in front of her. Mrs. Blue ties a string to a favorite toy. She places the toy out of Leslie's reach and helps her to pull the string to get her toy. After Leslie pulls it to herself, Mrs. Blue gives her a big hug and repeats the game.

Adaptation for the Visually Impaired.   Use a sound-making toy or a toy with a bell attached to it. Give your child physical assistance to reach for and grasp the object or toy.

Adaptation for the Physically Impaired.   Position your child so she can flex her arms and hands easily. If your child has difficulty grasping objects, try putting a mitten on her hand with Velcro attached to the palm, and attach a large piece of Velcro to the toy. When your child touches the Velcro on her mitten to the Velcro on the toy, it will stick. To help your child practice grasping, place a small ball in her hand and separate her fingers around the ball. For any type of grasping activity, use larger objects at first and move gradually to smaller objects.

Fun 'n' Food Games

These activities will give your child the opportunity to explore the tastes, textures, and scents of various foods and other items. These are the ingredients you'll need for this set of activities:

☆ Gelatin cut into squares

☆ Tray

☆ Blindfold

☆ Foods with a variety of tastes, smells, and textures

☆ Other items with scents

Here are a few Fun 'n' Food games you can play with your child.

Gelatin Mold Game

Make a batch of gelatin and cut it into squares. Stack a few squares on a tray in front of your child. She'll love the feel, smell, and taste of it. Mrs. Blue sometimes uses a slice of banana, a cracker, or a peeled apple slice to encourage Leslie to explore a variety of foods with different textures. Your young child should have at least a few upper and lower teeth for this game.

Gourmet Treats Game

When your child is able to eat table food, provide foods with different tastes and textures. Some examples: crackers (crisp), (yogurt (soft), marshmallows (sweet), dried fruit (chewy), peanut butter (sticky), or pickles (sour). Vary the temperature of foods—warm and cold. Use baby and junior foods for a younger child.

Guessing Game I

Prepare a meal that has several distinct tastes and smells. At mealtime, ask your child if she wants to play a special guessing game. Have her close her eyes and guess what food she is eating. She will be using three senses to make a guess: touch, smell, and taste. This game is for a child who has some language and/or can gesture by pointing or touching.

Guessing Game II

Blindfold your child or, if a blindfold is frightening, have her close her eyes. Let her smell a variety of pungent, but familiar, smells, one at a time. Ask her to guess each smell. If she is having trouble guessing, give her some clues. For example, with a lemon you could say, "It is yellow, round, and tastes sour." Here are some items with distinctive smells: strawberries, a freshly cut lemon, a freshly cut onion, an apple, peanut butter, or any type of flavored extract. Even if your child is unable to guess, she'll have fun just smelling a variety of items.

Fun 'n' Food Tips

Mrs. Blue lets Leslie suck on ice chips and popsicles. She keeps different foods separate rather than mixed together so tastes are distinct. She lets Leslie choose foods she would like to taste. You can give your child a wide variety of foods. Be adventurous; don't let your own dislikes influence your child. If your child refuses a food, don't force her. Try it again in a few weeks. You may also try preparing the food differently.

SAFETY NOTE

Be sure your pediatrician approves any new food to be added to your child's diet. Avoid any foods that your child is allergic to. Give your child only those foods that you are confident she can chew and will not choke on.

Adaptation for the Hearing Impaired. Use signs for names of foods.

Adaptation for the Physically Impaired. Assist child with touching and placing food in mouth. Instead of the gelatin activity, draw in vanilla pudding or mashed potatoes. Encourage your child to put her hands in the pudding, make finger and hand prints, and put her "pudding" finger into her mouth.

Shaving Cream Masterpiece Games

These activities will help your child explore and understand textures in three dimensions. These are the ingredients you'll need for this set of activities:

☆ Shaving cream or desert topping

☆ Food coloring

SAFETY NOTE

For children who may try to eat the shaving cream, substitute a whipped dessert topping, pudding, or yogurt.

These are a few Shaving Cream Masterpiece games you can play with your child.

Colored Shaving Cream Game

Turn your kitchen into an artist's workshop. Squirt shaving cream or dessert topping onto a smooth, slick surface such as the kitchen counter top, an acrylic cutting board, or a high chair tray and adds a few drops of food coloring. Your child can finger paint in the shaving cream, exploring with both hands for a while, then creating various shapes: circles, squares, triangles. She can draw faces, animals, and trees. Brothers, sisters, or friends can make this game twice as fun. In fact, you can make it a family affair. If your child is at an early developmental stage, use edible finger paint, such as whipped dessert topping or pudding.

Paint the Tub Game

Play the finger paint game during bathtime. Your child can paint the various parts of her body or the bath tiles. Shaving cream makes cleanup easy and fun. These games are great for helping a child explore the movement of her arms and legs. As your child moves her hands or feet, expand the movement. Move her whole arm or her whole leg, from the joint, in a circular motion, up and down, back and forth. Try this with only one arm or leg at a time, or both arms and legs together. This can also be a great outdoors game using a large plastic garbage bag or empty children's wading pool!

Adaptation for the Visually Impaired.   Use scented shaving cream or add a few drops of mint, lemon, or other highly scented cooking essence to the dessert topping.

Adaptation for the Physically Impaired.   Give your child the necessary physical guidance so that she can enjoy the cool, soft feelings of exploring the shaving cream.

Moving Sounds Games

These activities will help your child respond to and become familiar with various sounds in the environment and their location in space. They will also help her begin to understand cause/effect relationships. These are the ingredients you'll need for this set of activities:

☆ Musical mobile

☆ Ribbon or string bracelets with bells

☆ Toys that squeak or make other sounds

☆ 2 drums or pots

☆ Spoons

These are a few Moving Sounds games you can play.

Musical Mobile Game

Place a musical toy or mobile on either side of the crib or playpen for the child to see and hear. As she learns to reach, grasp, bat, and pull, use a mobile with a pull string to cause the mobile to make sounds when pulled. Soon she will learn that she can make sounds happen.

SAFETY NOTE

This activity should be closely supervised.

Jingle Jewelry Fun

Loosely tie bracelets made of elastic cord or ribbon and small bells to your child's wrists or ankles. Make sure bells are well secured. Your child will become more aware of her hands, arms, legs, and feet as she moves and the bells make pleasant, jingly sounds. If the sound is appealing to her, she will be motivated to move her limbs. If abrupt noises frighten your child, eliminate this activity until she becomes more tolerant of sounds. Continue to expose her to different sounds using favorite toys. Use brightly colored bracelets to attract her attention and create greater awareness.

SAFETY NOTE

Supervise this activity closely to make sure that little tongues
do not get caught in the bells and that bells do not come off.

Grab It Game

While your child is on her tummy or in a seated position, attract
her attention with a favorite sound-making or brightly colored toy.
Hold it to her right, then to her left and slightly above her. Hold
it close enough so that when the sound is made she can turn or lift
her head to see the toy. Encourage her to reach for and play with
it. She'll enjoy looking at it and exploring the sounds it makes when
she moves or squeezes the toy. Hold a rattle in front of her and move
it slowly around in a circle so she can follow it with her eyes. This
can be done with your child in various positions and with different
toys.

Bang the Drum Game

Using a pot and spoon or a toy drum, make music together. Take
turns imitating each other. Talk about the different rhythms and

sounds by using key words like "quiet" and "loud." Use your voice to imitate the rhythm. This is one of Leslie's favorite games. She loves to bang on Mother's big kettle with a wooden spoon.

Adaptation for the Hearing Impaired.   Observe the pitch and loudness of the sound that your child responds to in order to select appropriate sound-making toys. Let your child see and feel the toys and objects.

Adaptation for the Visually Impaired.   Present sounds for a little while longer to give your child a chance to respond. Give her the opportunity to touch and explore the objects and toys she hears.

Adaptation for the Physically Impaired.   Use slow, firm movements to assist your child in moving her arms and hands. If your child has increased muscle tone, make sure she is relaxed before manipulating her arms and legs.

Hear 'n' See Games

The purpose of these games is to help your child use her eyes, ears, and body to work together. These are the ingredients you'll need for this set of activities:

☆ Brightly colored toys and objects
☆ Sound-making toys and objects

Here are a few Hear 'n' See games you can play with your child.

Rattle Hear 'n' See Game

Place your child on her back or in a sitting position. Hold a sound-making object or toy, such as a rattle, musical animal, or ring of keys, in front of her. Shake the toy gently until your child looks at the toy. Smile and say, "You're looking at the rattle." Move the toy in a circle, horizontally, vertically, and in zigzags. Allow her to reach for, grasp, and shake or mouth the toy. Give her lots of smiles and cuddles as she watches the toy move above her.

Look 'n' Find Game

Place your child on her back. Hold two different brightly colored toys in front of your child so she can easily see them. First move one slowly so she can follow it with her eyes; then move the other one slowly. Alternate the movement of the toys to help her look from one to the other. Play this game with Dad or a brother or sister. Each person positions him- or herself on either side of your child. Attract her attention from one person to the other with the brightly colored toy. This will help to interest her in looking from one to the other.

Listen 'n' Look Game

Place your child on her back or in a sitting position in a baby seat. Shake a bell or rattle on either side of your child's head, but not so loudly as to frighten her. Ask her, "Where is the rattle?" Move slightly behind her so that she will move to see what she hears. A brother or sister can move around the room, not too far away, and ask her, "Where is Johnny?" When she looks, her brother or sister smiles and says, "There he is!"

Push-Ups Game

Place your child on her stomach. Dangle a brightly colored toy in front of her to interest her in lifting her head and pushing up with her hands. Once she lifts her head, raise the toy ever so slightly, but enough so that she will lift her head higher to see it. If this is difficult for your child, lightly stroke the back of her neck to stimulate neck muscles. Give your child a cuddle and talk to her about the toy. Rest a minute before trying this again.

Adaptation for the Hearing Impaired.   If your child does not seem to hear the sounds of certain toys or objects, try using a toy that lights up or has moving parts.

Adaptation for the Visually Impaired.   Use objects and toys with interesting textures and sounds. Use sound-making toys for a little longer time so your child has ample opportunity to hear and respond to the sound. Help your child move toward the object by gently turning her head and guiding her hand to reach out and touch the object. To help your child visually attend to and follow an object, use a flashlight or penlight with colored filters or cellophane in a dimly lit room. Hold the light about 8 to 10 inches from your child, and move the light slowly to attract her attention.

Talking Sounds Games

These activities will help your child develop important language skills and encourage her to imitate sounds and words. These are the ingredients you'll need for this set of activities:

- ☆ Pictures of animals
- ☆ Songs and nursery rhymes

Here are a few Talking Sounds games you can play with your child.

Name Game

Say your child's name as you pick her up, rock her, change her clothing, or bathe her. Talk to her and cuddle her so that she hears your voice, looks at you, and feels secure in her world.

Happy Songs Game

Sing songs and repeat nursery rhymes over and over again to her. These games can be played at bedtime. Use favorite songs and rhymes from your own childhood and songs of your faith or culture. Use happy songs. (See chapter 6 of this book for some songs.)

Animal Sounds Game

One of Leslie's favorite games is Animal Sounds. Mrs. Blue shows Leslie a picture of a cow and says, "This is a cow." She makes a mooing sound. Leslie tries to imitate the sound and Mrs. Blue gives her the picture. They play the game with pictures of all sorts of animals that Mrs. Blue cuts out of magazines. You can enjoy making funny animal noises with your child, too.

Tube Talk Game

Have a brother or sister talk to your child through a cardboard paper towel tube. Encourage your child to talk back through the tube. Ask the brother or sister to imitate the child. Try singing songs or making funny sounds.

Adaptation for the Hearing Impaired.   Even if your child does not hear well, continue to talk to her, making sure she can see your face. Play music and expose her to environmental sounds. Even if she has very limited hearing or does not hear at all, she will feel sound vibrations. Place her hand on your throat so she can feel the vibrations of the sounds you make.

Adaptation for the Physically Impaired.   Place your child in a comfortable position. Use gestures and facial expressions to help her understand that sound communicates meaning from one person to another.

Body Part Games

These activities will improve your child's self-image and help her to learn the names of parts of the body. These are the ingredients you'll need for this set of activities:

☆ Mirror

☆ Comb or brush

☆ Baby doll

☆ Small blanket or dish towel

Here are a few Body Part games you can play with your child.

Name That Part Game

Point to and name the parts of your child's body, such as head, hair, eyes, ears, nose, mouth, tummy, arms, hands, fingers, and legs. Touch the parts as you say them and help her to touch them. Ask your child to point to specific body parts on herself, her brother or sister, and you. If your child is talking, ask her to name the different body parts. Say to her, "Point to your nose," or "What are you touching?" If she has trouble answering, say, "Is that your nose or your foot?" Make this a family game and be sure to play it while getting ready for bed or taking a bath.

Mirror Images Game

In this activity Leslie and Mrs. Blue sit in front of a mirror so that Leslie can see her reflection. Mrs. Blue points to Leslie in the mirror and says, "I see Leslie. [pause] Where is Leslie? [pause] Find Leslie." Leslie points to herself in the mirror and smiles. Once Leslie can do this, Mrs. Blue touches Leslie's mouth and says, "Mouth, here is Leslie's mouth." Mrs. Blue helps Leslie find her nose, mouth, ears, and other body parts in the mirror. They also have a lot of fun playing Peek-a-Boo in front of the mirror. Even if your child cannot understand all of the words you use in these games, she will become aware of language, sounds, concepts, and the associations you make between actions and words.

Doll Fun Game

During bathtime Mrs. Blue uses Leslie's favorite waterproof doll to help her learn about the parts of the body. They talk about the different body parts as they wash and dry the doll's face, arms, hands, legs, and feet. Your child's brother or sister can help bathe and dry the doll with your child, making bathtime even more fun and interesting.

Body-Does Game

Use your child's doll to make a fun game of learning what function goes with different parts of the body. Hold the doll on your lap and use your hand to cover the part where "dolly eats," "dolly talks," "dolly sees," "dolly hears," "dolly smells," "dolly walks," and so on. After you have gone over this, ask your child to cover the part where "dolly sees." Ask her what part she is covering. Go through this with each of the various body parts. This game is fun to play as a family with or without the doll.

Adaptation for the Hearing Impaired. Use sign language or gestures to identify the various body parts, and make sure you encourage your child to look at the body parts you are describing.

Adaptation for the Visually Impaired. Help your child touch and explore the parts of the body you are pointing to or talking about.

Texture Box Games

These activities will help children "see" with their fingers and describe objects they touch. These are the ingredients you will need to make a texture box:

☆ Container—shoe or other cardboard box, small plastic tub

☆ Packing tape

☆ Textured items: oatmeal, rice, dried beans, macaroni, cotton, Styrofoam packing pieces, feathers, cereal, dry leaves

☆ Tools and toys: brush, spoon, ball, cup, toy car, truck, doll

☆ Small plastic containers

☆ Large cardboard square

☆ Yarn

☆ Glue

Here are a few Texture Box games you can play with your child.

Combinations Texture Box Game

To make a texture box, Mrs. Blue fills the box or tub with one or a combination of the ingredients from the textured items list, after sealing the bottom of the container with packing tape. As Leslie fingers the materials in the box, Mrs. Blue uses words like "soft," "rough," or "prickly" to describe the textures. She also uses descriptive vocal cues to make the game more fun. For example, she says the word "rough" in a low, rough voice. She always uses the same word to describe the same texture. When you first play this game, begin with one texture. When your child understands, combine it with others. Take turns with brothers or sisters leading the game. Using items with similar textures, repeat the descriptive words. Your child will learn that you are describing the feel of the texture and not naming the item itself.

Some children will be hesitant about touching unfamiliar textures. Gently encourage your child to explore, or have siblings provide an example. It may also be helpful to demonstrate each game first. If your child dislikes a particular texture, try another.

Fill the Cup Game

Take a spoon and fill a cup with any ingredient from the texture box. Pour it out. Use words such as "fill," "full," "pour," and "empty" to describe the game. Ask your child to copy your actions. By holding oatmeal in your hand and letting it run through your fingers, illustrate "full" and "empty." Allow your child to explore and play freely with the oatmeal and various containers.

Touch 'n' Find Game

Hide two small toys (for example, a ball and a car) under textured items in a box. Ask your child to get the ball without looking into the box. Give her clues like, "The ball is round and smooth." When she finds it, clap your hands, give her a hug, and let her play with it. Talk about the ball and how it is different from the car. Play the game again. Add toys as your child progresses. Add as many toys as your child can find. Use favorite toys—this will help encourage your child to find them. Let your child hide a toy and tell you to look for it. It's not easy!

Toy Find Game

Leslie loves to play with cardboard boxes, which can be more fun than expensive toys. Mrs. Blue hides favorite toys in a box of foam packing beads, paper balls (cut or rip grocery bags and crunch into little balls to fill box), or leaves. Give your child and her brother or sister each a turn to find a toy and then hide it again.

Box Fun Game

Another way to use a cardboard box is to fill it with one of the ingredients from the Toy Find. Make sure the box is large enough so that a brother or sister can play too. Let your children explore the contents of the box—possibly putting just an arm or leg in first. Sit your child in the box after removing her shirt, shoes, and socks. Many children love this game.

Beans and Boxes Game

Punch holes in the lid of an empty shoe box or oatmeal container. Give the box to your child along with a plastic bowl filled with dried beans or macaroni. Let her fill the box with the beans, empty it, and start again. Use words such as "empty," "full," "in," and "out" while playing this game. If your child is younger or does not have sufficient motor skills to pick up small objects like beans, take the lid off the box and let her fill it up with various small toys and textured objects that are easier for her to manipulate. After the box is full, empty it and start again!

Feely Board Game

Glue pieces of yarn onto a large piece of cardboard, dividing it into eight squares. Glue materials of various textures in each square. Keep duplicates of each of the materials. Help your child match the textured items to the same material on the feely board. Help her explore with her fingers and talk about how each item feels. Textured items could include cotton, feathers, sandpaper, buttons, carpet squares, and velour.

SAFETY NOTE

Supervise Texture Box activities closely so children do not mouth or swallow objects. Special supervision must be given to children at the mouthing stage. Do not leave your child alone for any Texture Box activities.

Adaptation for the Hearing Impaired.   Use signs for the objects, and be sure to use some objects for which your child has already learned the signs.

Adaptation for the Visually Impaired. Encourage your child to take her time and explore a variety of materials. Describe the textures and shapes of the material.

Hide 'n' Find Games

Hide 'n' Find activities will help your child understand that objects she can no longer see can still exist. They will also encourage her to find hidden objects. These are the ingredients you'll need for this set of activities:

- ☆ Mirror
- ☆ Hand towel or small blanket
- ☆ Ball or other favorite small toy
- ☆ Box with pictures glued to it

Here are a few Hide 'n' Find games you can play with your child.

Peek-a-Boo Game

Peek-a-Boo is one of the most common Hide 'n' Find games. Make sure Mom, brothers, sisters, and Dad join in the fun. For variety use a mirror and small blanket for Peek-a-Boo. Another fun game is, "Where Is the Baby?" The adult covers the child's face with both hands or a hand towel and says, "Where is the baby?" Then the adult removes hands or towel and with a big smile says, "There she is!"

Where Am I Game

Hide behind a chair, letting your child see part of you. Call out, "Where am I? Come and find me." Hug her when she does. Repeat the game. When she wants to hide, act surprised when you find her. Vary the game by hiding a favorite stuffed animal. Place your child on the floor near a brother, sister, or another child. Say, "I am going to hide Sally," and then place a hand towel over Sally's head. Ask, "Where is Sally?" When Sally pulls the towel off, everyone says, "There is Sally." Repeat with other children in turn. After playing this game a few times, the children will anticipate whose turn is next.

Hide-a-Toy Game

Show your child a special toy. Let her touch it while you hold it in your hand. Have her watch as you place the toy behind you. Ask, "Where did the toy go?" If she does not look for it, show her the toy again and encourage her to find it. When she finds it, say, "Great! You found the toy," and let her play with it. Hide it in other places, such as in your shirt pocket or under a towel, and let her discover it. Enjoy the game with her and respond enthusiastically when she succeeds.

Toy Find Game

Hold a favorite toy in front of your child until she sees and reaches for it. Cover it quickly with a small blanket or dish towel, then ask her to find the toy. When you introduce this game, leave a little of the toy showing to remind her that the toy is still there. Once she catches on to this game, wrap the toy in the blanket, give it to her, and let her delight in unwrapping it and finding her toy. Reverse the game—place the toy in front of her so that she can cover it and you can find it. You can also play this game by placing the toy in a box, a bag, or a pot with a lid.

Box Drop Game

Make a small hole in the top of a box and a larger hole on one side near the bottom of the box. Show your child how to drop a favorite toy into the top of the box. Ask her if she can still see it. Ask her to find it, and show her the larger hole where she can put her hand through and pull out the toy. Once she understands the game, she will begin looking through the larger hole once she has dropped the toy into the box.

Search 'n' Find Game

Leslie likes to play Search 'n' Find. She sits on the floor and Mrs. Blue shows her a box with a big picture of a familiar object or face pasted on the side. She turns the picture away and asks Leslie to find it. Mrs. Blue keeps reminding Leslie of the picture by saying the name of the object or person. She encourages Leslie to move the box around to find the picture. Mrs. Blue cheers and claps when Leslie finds the picture.

Who Is Missing? Game

Have the family sit in a circle; ask one member to leave the room. Encourage your child to name the person who is missing. Family members take turns being the missing person. Vary the number of persons out of the room at one time.

Hide 'n' Seek Game

Ask your child to turn around and not peek. Hide a favorite toy under one of two or three very different-sized containers or very different objects, such as an oatmeal container and a dish towel. Ask her to find the toy. Once she finds it, try the game again, keeping the toy in the same spot but under a different container. Increase the number of hiding containers once your child masters the game. Use your imagination to vary this hide-'n'-seek game. Make it simpler or more challenging depending on your child's ability level.

Adaptation for the Hearing Impaired. Use signs as needed and make sure your child's visual attention is on the object.

Adaptation for the Visually Impaired.   Hide something that makes noise, like an alarm clock, kitchen timer, music box, or portable radio. This will help give your child a clue to find the toy. Use brightly colored, prominently shaped toys and objects.

Adaptation for the Physically Impaired.   Position your child so she can easily reach the object and remove the cover that is hiding it. Watch for signals from her eyes that indicate she wants to reach for the object. Give her the physical assistance she needs to reach for and hold the object or remove the cover. Use Velcro as suggested in Stretch 'n' Reach activites.

Flashlight Games

Flashlight activities help children focus their eyes on a single object against a contrasting background. These are the ingredients you'll need for this set of activities:

- ☆ Flashlight
- ☆ Blanket
- ☆ Card table, kitchen table, or large cardboard box
- ☆ Familiar pictures
- ☆ Toys and other familiar objects

Here are two Flashlight Games you can play with your child.

Spotlight Game

Place a blanket over the table or box to make a little house for you and your child to play in. Place two to five toys or familiar objects inside this house. Help your child hold a flashlight to spotlight the toys. Talk about each toy. Next, ask her to find the object or toy you mention. Reverse roles and let your child tell you which toy to find. For an older child, try this game using pictures of favorite toys or foods. Hang two to five pictures inside the house.

Cat and Mouse Game

You and your child each have a flashlight. Your child shines the light around a darkened room. Try to follow the light with your flashlight. Reverse roles and ask your child to follow your light.

Adaptation for the Visually Impaired.   Use pictures and objects that are brightly colored or shiny or make a noise.

Grab Bag Games

Try these activities to help your child learn about and group similar objects and to understand the concepts of "same" and "different." Grab Bag games will also help your child identify objects by touch and name. These are the ingredients you'll need for this set of activities:

- ☆ Bag or shoe box
- ☆ Buttons
- ☆ Crayons
- ☆ Familiar objects
- ☆ Hard and soft objects, such as a rock and a cotton pad

☆ Different-colored objects, such as small colored blocks and pieces of colored paper

☆ Paper plates

Here are two Grab Bag games you can play with your child.

Grouping Game

Fill a bag or shoe box with buttons and crayons or any two groups of objects that look very different. Place two paper plates in front of your child. Ask your child to reach in the bag and pull out an object. Help her to label the object ("You have a button") and then place it on a paper plate. Ask her to pull out another object. Again, help her to identify it and to place it on the first plate if it is the same and on the other plate if it is different. Continue to have your child sort the objects until the bag is empty. Use words such as "same" and "different." You can also play this game with hard and soft objects, heavy and light objects, and objects that go together, like a comb and brush, shoe and sock, or toothbrush and toothpaste.

Family Guessing Game

Place a group of assorted familiar objects in front of your child along with a paper bag. Have your child fill the bag with the objects, naming them as she puts them in the bag one at a time. Each member of the family gets a turn to reach in the bag, pull out an object, guess what it is, and name it. Blindfold each member of the family when it is his or her turn. If a blindfold is too frightening for your child, help her to put her hand in the bag without looking or ask her to close her eyes. If this game is too difficult for your child, give her a choice after she pulls her object from the bag: "Is it a spoon or a ball?" To add some fun to this game, award pennies every time someone guesses correctly. This is also an enjoyable birthday party game. These activities will help your child to explore objects with her hands and to use objects and toys that have distinct physical characteristics.

Adaptation for the Physically Impaired.   Position your child so she can reach the objects. Use objects of appropriate size and shape so your child can grasp them.

Shake, Rattle, 'n' Roll Games

These games and activities will help your child explore different sounds, identify "same" and "different" sounds, and develop the concept that objects still exist even when out of sight. These are the ingredients you'll need for this set of activities:

☆ Small blanket or a towel

☆ Small plastic containers, such as empty spice or lotion bottles, two plastic cups with their mouths taped together, or cardboard tubes from wrapping paper

☆ Small items found around the house or outdoors, such as paper clips, pebbles, coins, rice, macaroni, small blocks, or beads (include lightweight items that make quiet sounds as well as heavy items that make loud sounds)

SAFETY NOTE

Make sure tops of jars are securely sealed so there is no risk of the child swallowing the objects.

Here are a few Shake, Rattle, 'n' Roll games you can play with your child.

Shaker Toys Game

Mrs. Blue fills four containers with different items found around the house. The containers are half filled so the items can move freely. Leslie makes sounds by shaking, moving, and rolling the containers.

Hide the Sounds Game

Once your child has explored the shaker, wrap one in a blanket. Sit next to your child on the floor and move the wrapped blanket around so that she can hear the rattle even though she cannot see it. Ask your child to unwrap the rattle or pull the blanket away so she can find the toy and play with it.

Match the Sound Game

Later, play matching sounds. Place three to four very different sound-making shakers on individual paper plates or napkins. (This helps keep them separate.) Place a duplicate group of shakers, which makes the same sounds, nearby. Ask your child to shake one of the original shakers and then identify the matching sound from the second group of shakers.

Find the Sound Game

For an even more advanced version of this game, line up two to four different shakers on the floor. All should make very different sounds. Ask your child to select one, shake it, and put it back. Change the order of the shakers and encourage her to find the "same" shaker. When she does, let her become the leader of the game and mix the shakers for you. Play the game again, but this time ask her to find the "soft" or "quiet" shaker, then the "loud" shaker.

Water Tap Game

Fill glasses with varying amounts of water. Use an unsharpened pencil or chopstick to tap out various notes and rhythms. If your child has good hand coordination, she can tap by herself; otherwise hold her hand and guide her. This activity should be done only under direct supervision.

Adaptation for the Hearing Impaired.   Shake, Rattle, 'n' Roll games are not appropriate for your child if she is severely/profoundly deaf. If your child has only some degree of hearing, these games will still be very difficult. Omit the use of shakers, and instead play Match the Sound using very loud and varied sounds, such as drums or bells. Use sounds that create distinct vibrations.

Adaptation for the Physically Impaired.   Use containers your child can easily grasp, or make adaptive containers especially for your child.

All Kinds of Sounds Games

These games will help familiarize your child with everyday sounds, including voices. They will encourage talking, listening, and developing the ability to compare loud and soft sounds. These games are particularly appropriate for the whole family. These are the ingredients you'll need for this set of activities:

☆ Tape recorder with microphone or prerecorded sound effects

☆ Recorded sounds, including voices of family members and/or friends, airplane taking off, running water, fire engine passing by, clapping, typewriter, vacuum cleaner, piano, doorbell and telephone ringing, TV, dog barking or other animal sounds, car honking, and other familiar sounds

☆ Record player

☆ Records or cassettes

Here are a few All Kinds of Sounds games you can play with your child.

House Sounds Game

Start simply. Prerecord voices of family members and other familiar sounds. Spread pictures that correspond to the sounds on a table or floor. Before starting the game, make certain you discuss each picture. Play each sound, then stop the recorder or record player and ask your child to identify the sound and locate its corresponding picture. Give everyone in the family a turn. Each member who guesses the right sound gets to keep the corresponding picture.

Family Sound Track Game

Have fun with the tape recorder. Record different family members—talking, singing, imitating animals. Play each sound back and enjoy all the different sound effects you can make together.

Loud 'n' Soft Sounds Game

Play a record or tape and ask family members to identify loud and soft sounds. Play the tape again and have everyone cover their ears for loud sounds and place fingers over their lips for quiet sounds.

Adaptation for the Hearing Impaired.   All Kinds of Sounds Games should be omitted if your child has a severe or profound hearing loss. If your child has a mild to moderate hearing loss, try House Sounds Game and Loud 'n' Soft Sounds Game, using very distinct sounds and sounds that cause vibrations.

Adaptation for the Visually Impaired.   Help your child explore the various house sounds she is listening to. Make sure she feels the textures, shapes, sizes, and vibrations of the different sound-makers.

Sensory Stimulation for All Ages

These are only a few of the activities you can do with your child to stimulate sensory development. Use your imagination and draw upon your childhood memories to create your own activities. Remember that even though sensory learning begins at the earliest developmental stages, children of all ages continue to learn through their senses. Make sure you give your child plenty of sensory experiences, regardless of her developmental stage.

Chapter 3

EXPLORING
THE WORLD OF
MOVEMENT

Simon Says. Simon Says, "Stop!" Simon Says, "Go!" It's a simple game. But for many children with handicaps, making the body move the way they want it to can be as difficult as climbing a mountain. Developing body awareness, motor coordination, and general motor abilities is an art—an art of rhythm and movement. Some children with disabilities can move easily, while others have difficulty because of motor and physical problems. With each movement, a young child strengthens muscles, develops balance, learns to relate to his physical environment, and gains a greater sense of how his body moves. Every child needs to make these important motor skills discoveries; they are the foundation for future physical, social, and academic development. Whatever a child's disability, he needs to participate at some level in physical activities.

The motor abilities that the nondisabled child develops through spontaneous play can be experienced by the child with a motor impairment through adapted and guided play. Begin by observing your child. Watch him as he moves through his world. Learn his strengths and weaknesses. Let his body teach you the games it requires to grow and become strong. If the games are too simple, make them more challenging. If they are too difficult, simplify. Give the child an opportunity to explore his physical abilities. The most important aspect of each game is that it be fun! Sound simple? It can be, but rarely is. For example, sit in a chair and kick a ball that's placed in front of you. If you have highly developed motor skills and reflexes, this task appears very easy. Now do it again, but this time identify all of the isolated movements and coordination commands your brain sends to your body to tell it to kick the ball: "Bend the knee. Bring the leg back. Swing the leg forward—not too hard! Keep looking at the ball to make contact. Touch it!" It takes more work than you thought.

The child with a disability knows this, for he often struggles to get the body and brain to work together. Because his brain may require more time to interpret what his body should do, his responses may be delayed or slower than another child's. Give him the time and support he needs to understand and organize information. If your child has a physical disability, assist him through the activities when possible. Modify activities to focus on the able parts of his body. When your child has difficulty with a particular activity, try the activity yourself. See what is involved. Isolate the parts of the activity he needs assistance with.

Through Walk 'n' Roll, Crawl 'n' Stroll, and Build 'n' Scoot games, parents, brothers, sisters, and grandparents can help your child strengthen muscles, develop balance, relate to the physical environment, and gain a greater awareness of how his body moves. Most important, these activities are designed to promote family fun!

The Green Family Plays Walk 'n' Roll, Crawl 'n' Stroll, Build 'n' Scoot Games

Like any 5-year-old, Johnny Green likes to play, but he is hesitant about trying games or activities that involve large muscle movement. Johnny has a mild hearing loss and perceptual-motor difficulties. He is unsure of his body, and simple movements can throw him off balance. Therefore, movement can be very frightening to him. In addition to his fear of getting hurt, he often becomes frustrated and embarrassed when he cannot do an activity easily.

You can often find Johnny sitting quietly in a corner or staring out the window. He enjoys sitting on his daddy's lap and having stories read to him, or listening to music with his 8-year-old sister Kathy, who is very good at making him laugh. It's a real challenge, though, for the Green family to find active movement games that make Johnny put aside his fears. But they do.

"Come on, everybody. Let's play follow the leader!" Mr. Green says to the family. Johnny stays in his chair by the window as the family begins the game. Soon the giggling and fun are too much for him to ignore. He quietly joins the others.

SAFETY NOTE

Motor activities should not be used with a physically handicapped child without the supervision or guidance of a physical or occupational therapist.

Rock 'n' Roll Games

These games will help your child develop important gross motor movement, large muscle coordination, and a sense of the body's position in space. A sturdy, cozy blanket is the only ingredient you will need to enjoy this set of activities.

Rock 'n' Roll Game

Get ready to rock 'n' roll! Have your child lie on his back on a blanket. Place both your hands on the sides of your child's body and gently rock him back and forth as you sing one of his favorite songs.

Kiddie Rock Game

Place the very young child in the center of the blanket. Ask other family members to hold the edges of the blanket and gently lift it with the child lying in the middle. Sway him back and forth while singing "Rock-a-Bye-Baby" or another favorite song. Surround him with happy talk and smiles. If he appears frightened, gently rock him in your arms instead of in the blanket.

Kiddie Tug Game

Have your child lie on his back in the center of the blanket. Gather up two corners of the blanket and pull him slowly across the room. Challenge your child by having him sit up, but be careful not to let him fall.

Jelly Roll Game

To help encourage your child to roll, place him on his back with his chin tucked into his chest, take his right arm and stretch it over his head, and bend his left leg at the knee. Finally, turn him in the direction of the stretched hand and give him a little push at the hip. Now try this with the left arm outstretched and the right knee bent, rolling your child to the left. Always encourage your child to initiate motor activities with both sides of his body.

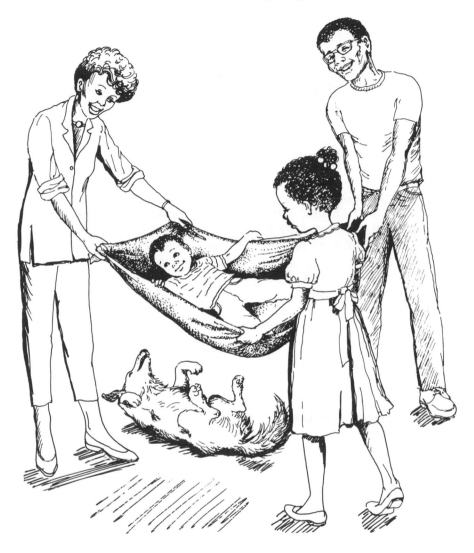

Towel Roll Game

Wrap your child in a towel or blanket and then pull one end of the blanket very gently so that he rolls out onto a pad or soft rug. Johnny and Kathy especially enjoy this game. Kathy calls Johnny her "big yummy jelly roll," and Johnny giggles as she gently rolls him onto the living room carpet.

Adaptation for the Physically Impaired.   With your child on his back, gently hold his feet and alternate movement back and forth like the movements used for riding a bike. Repeat this procedure with his arms. If your child has increased muscle tone, this will assist him with loosening up his body and with separation of movement for the two sides of the body.

Copy Me Games

The purpose of these activities is to encourage learning through imitation. Imitating others is an important skill and will enhance your child's ability to learn many other skills, such as eating with utensils, talking, and kicking a ball. Drums and sticks or pots and safe kitchen utensils (e.g., spoons) are the only ingredients you will need to enjoy these activities.

See Me, Copy Me Game

Use your baby's or young child's lead for playing a game of See Me, Copy Me. Parents, a brother, or a sister imitate the different sounds he makes and the various movements he uses to explore his body. Talk to him about what he is doing. Even if he cannot understand words, he will enjoy the sound of your voices. Place him on your lap in front of a mirror so that both of you can be seen in the mirror. Tap on the mirror to attract his attention. Guide his hand over your face and then his face while naming the various body parts. Play Peek-a-Boo or "Where is (child's name)?"

Cooking Fun Game

When you are cooking, take a spoon, bang on a pan, and tell your child, "Follow me," or "Bang, bang, bang." When he does, acknowledge what he is doing. You can tap on a table, clap your hands, stomp your feet, or think of other noise-making and rhythm games that you and your child can play together. Cook together. When you stir in a pot or bowl, give your child a wooden spoon and a bowl with food in it. Let him watch you stir. Encourage him to copy your action.

Follow the Leader Game

Play Follow the Leader using a variety of different actions. Let your child be the leader while the rest of the family imitates what he does.

Mirror Image Game

Mr. Green and Johnny stand facing each other. Mr. Green tells Johnny to copy his hand movements, but not to touch hands. They start with very simple, slow movements and build to quicker, more complex movements.

Adaptation for the Hearing Impaired. Use sign language for labeling simple objects and making requests.

Adaptation for the Visually Impaired. Encourage all tactile or touching exploration that your child initiates. If he does not initiate, guide his hands over the different objects you are playing with together.

Everybody Do This Just Like Me Game

This game will help your child learn to follow simple directions through imitation and will aid in the development of gross motor skills. You need only family and friends to play.

Each family member takes a turn being leader. Each leader uses this chant:

Everybody do this, do this, do this.
Everybody do this just like me.
(The leader performs some action, such as hand clapping).
Everybody (clap hands, clap hands, clap hands).
Everybody (clap hands) just like me!

Each new leader leads the chant in a sing-song fashion. Each time the verse is chanted, the leader demonstrates a different action. All join in to copy the action and sing the chant. Actions can include stomping feet, touching different parts of the body, hopping on one foot, or rolling over. Use your imagination!

Follow the Leader and Simon Says are two well-known variations of this game.

Adaptation for the Visually Impaired. If your child is blind, describe your actions and physically guide him through the activity so he can feel what he should imitate. Activities producing distinctive sounds will help give him needed feedback.

Adaptation for the Physically Impaired. Your child may not be able to imitate your posture. If not, place him in a comfortable, ready-to-play position, which may be lying, sitting, or standing with or without support, and guide him through the movements.

Climb 'n' Roll Games

These games will help your child further develop body awareness by rolling and crawling up and down an incline. These are the ingredients you'll need for this set of activities:

☆ Mattress

☆ Target objects, such as plastic bowling pins, plastic milk cartons, or empty shoe boxes

Here are a few Climb 'n' Roll games you can play with your child.

Roll Over Game

Place your baby or young child on his back and sit behind him. Hold a favorite toy just above his face. While he is watching, slowly move it toward the top of his head at his side, encouraging him to look at it while you move it. When he turns over to try to see and reach it, let him have the toy. Give him a hug and lots of smiles. Soon your child will roll over with the aim of getting the toys and objects he wants to play with.

Mountain Climbing Game

Slant a mattress off the side of a bed, forming a ramp. Begin "mountain climbing" by crawling up the slope. Encourage your child to follow closely behind. You may need to support the space under the mattress with a bolster. Talk to your child about climbing the mountain. When he reaches the top, help him roll back down, huffing and puffing as you go, saying, "Down the mountain we go." Repeat several times.

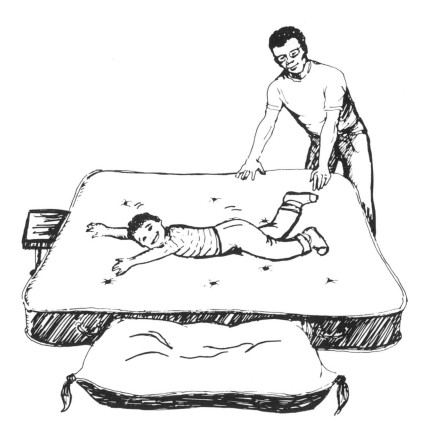

Body Bowl Game

Mr. Green places target objects at the bottom of an inclined mattress. Johnny and Kathy roll down the mattress and knock over the targets with their bodies. You can demonstrate how much fun this can be. Allow your child to explore freely the various ways he can move up and down the incline.

Adaptation for the Visually Impaired.   Use sound-making targets.

SAFETY NOTE

If your child is physically impaired, this activity should not be used without the supervision or guidance of a physical or occupational therapist.

Creep 'n' Crawl Trail Games

These games will encourage motor planning and help your child develop the ability to vary motor patterns and understand how objects relate to himself and others in space. These are the ingredients you'll need for this set of activities:

☆Yarn, rope (40 to 60 feet long), or masking tape

☆Mats, open floor space, or grassy area

Here are two Creep 'n' Crawl Trail games you can play with your child.

Creep 'n' Crawl Toy Game

Place your child either in a sitting position or on his tummy on the floor. Put his favorite toy or object on the floor nearby. When he begins to creep or crawl towards his toy, encourage him to get it with lots of smiles. As your child gets better at crawling, move the toy further away so he has to go a little farther to get it. At first your child may just rock on his hands and knees before he begins to move by creeping or crawling. Encourage this position with lots of praise. Move the objects closer so he can balance his weight on one hand and reach for the toy with the other. Scoop him up in your arms and play with him before starting again.

Crawling Trail Game

This is one of the Green family's favorite activities. Using colored yarn, plain rope, or masking tape, Mr. Green outlines a winding trail on the floor or grassy area. Johnny and Kathy crawl along the trail on their hands and knees. When you first introduce this game, you might want to demonstrate first. Crawl next to your child and show him the various ways to creep and crawl. You can use a "commando-style" crawl—lying on the tummy and using arms in an arm-over-arm pulling motion—or with upper body upright, follow the trail by walking on your knees. If necessary, arrange the trail so that you can creep beside a reluctant child. The Greens arrange the trail around, under, over, and between large pieces of household furniture, cardboard boxes, or other objects. Talk to your child about his movement around, under, or over objects.

Adaptation for the Physically Impaired.   Use a scooter board for a child unable to crawl; encourage him to use his arms and/or legs to propel himself. A brother or sister can pull him through the trail on a wagon or scooter board if he cannot push himself. (See instructions for using and making scooter boards at the end of this chapter.)

Eyes 'n' Hands Games

These games will help your child to develop important eye-hand coordination and fine motor skills, enhance imitation skills, and learn about taking turns and playing cooperatively. Some of the following games will also assist your child in learning the difference between objects by ordering them according to size or shape. These are the ingredients you'll need for this set of activities:

☆ Objects for building and stacking: colored cubes, small blocks, sponges, pillows, empty pint-size milk cartons, shoe boxes

☆ Objects for nesting: commercial nesting toys, paper cups, oatmeal container, plastic bowls, or cans of various sizes

☆ Stacking ring

☆ Pie pan

☆ Play dough

☆ Cupcake pan

See specific activities for additional ingredients

These are a few Eyes 'n' Hands games you can play with your child.

Yum Yum Cupcake Fun Game

Use a cupcake pan and play dough. Explain to your child that you are going to pretend to make cupcakes. Help him roll the play dough into cupcake shapes. Once he is finished making the cupcakes, he places them in the cupcake pan and serves them to his favorite dolls and stuffed animals. Mr. Green and Johnny like to use peanut butter, granola, or graham cracker crumbs and raisins to make real, miniature cupcake treats for the whole family. Help your child learn to pick up raisins using his thumb and forefinger.

Scooper Game

Cut off the bottom of a large, clean, plastic milk or bleach bottle. Turn it upside down and give it to your child to use as a scooper to scoop up ping-pong balls or crumpled newspaper balls. Have a bucket nearby into which he can dump the balls.

Tower Power Game

Place blocks in a bucket and ask your child to take them out. Using three blocks, show your child how to build a tower and knock it down. As your child begins to understand building and knocking down, add more blocks to the game. Help him take turns with a sister or brother as they build a tower together. Vary the objects used by including objects for building and stacking (see ingredients list above). Always make sure that your children have unstructured time to play with blocks and containers in their own way. Give your child the time and encouragement to explore different ways to play with these objects. Add to the fun by imitating your child's way of playing.

Building and Nesting Game

Use two or three different-sized containers (from the suggestions in the ingredients list) that fit one inside the other. Help your child build a tower with the largest object placed upside down for the bottom and the smallest on the top. Knock the tower down and encourage your child to build it again. Play this game differently by placing the small containers inside the next larger ones. Help your child pull or dump them out. Use words like "little," "big," "in," "out," "top," and "bottom," to describe the objects and what you are doing. A stacking ring toy is also useful. When your child is first learning to stack the rings, it is not important that he place them according to size. Just play with the rings, stacking and building, and talk about what you both are doing. Your child might need some time and practice with these toys to be able to stack them by size.

Surprise Jars Game

Use two to five plastic containers or jars of varied sizes, with both pop-on and twist-on lids. Put small toys or favorite food treats into the containers. Place the various containers in front of your child. Shake them, explain that there is a surprise inside, and ask him how he can get the surprise out. Help him get started by popping off one of the lids with your fingers. Encourage him to open the next one to see what surprise awaits. After all the lids are off, and the treats are removed, help him use his fingers to grasp the small items and refill the jars. When the containers are filled, help him put the lids back onto the right containers. Use fewer containers to make the game easier.

Train Express Game

Use two duplicate groups of three or four different-shaped blocks. Place one group in front of you and one group in front of your child.

Ask your child to help you make a train. Start the train by placing a block in a set place and asking your child to find the same block from his group and put it right next to yours. Continue until you have used all the blocks. Point out to your child that you are building a train together and taking turns. Remind him of the blocks he used to help make the train. Let him decide which blocks to start putting away. Once your child understands this game, invite Dad, brother, and sister to join the fun to make it a real group effort. As your child gets older and develops his skills, the train will become more sophisticated. Mr. and Mrs. Green, Kathy, and Johnny have great fun creating intricate trains, bridges, and roads.

Happy Face Game

Use a round cake pan and 18 one-inch blocks. Explain to your child that together you are going to make a happy face with the blocks. Use the cake pan to help your child form the circle by placing 10 blocks around the outside of the pan. Remove the pan from the center and show your child how he has made a circle for the face. Ask him what he needs to place in the circle to make a happy face. Use the remaining blocks for eyes, nose, and, of course, a big, happy smile.

Shoe Box Tower Game

Cut out a shoe box so that standing it on end provides a corner for building a tall tower with 1-inch cube blocks. This will give support, helping your child to build a tower successfully. Use this game to help him learn to take turns with a brother or sister. Begin by demonstrating to your child how to match the corner of the block to the corner of the shoe box. After the tower is built, have fun knocking it down and starting over again.

Tower Power Game

Use a variety of assorted blocks, boxes, containers, toy cars, and small plastic or wooden toy people. As your child develops in areas of fine and gross motor skills as well as imagination, the family can help him create city towers, roads, bridges, houses, and trains. Make a road with twisting parallel lines of yarn. He can use his favorite toy cars and people to make his city come to life. His make-believe stories will add to the fun for the whole family, but he might need ideas and encouragement to get his interesting stories started.

Clothespin Squeeze

Use a coffee can or large empty container with smooth edges, and clothespins. (Make sure the clothespin springs are weak; otherwise they may be too difficult for your child to open.) Place all the clothespins in the can and ask your child to take one out and snap it onto the rim of the can. Show your child how to open and close the clothespin using thumb and forefinger. Help him to place his finger on it and squeeze to open. To make the game more challenging, use clear tape to attach 1/2-inch pieces of colored construction paper near the rim of the can. Color-code the clothespins for a game of matching colors. Johnny and Kathy like playing this game, but instead of matching colors, Johnny matches the letters of the alphabet. Kathy prints upper- and lower-case letters onto small posterboard squares and tapes them to clothespins. With a little help from Kathy, Johnny matches up the alphabet-coded clothespins to letters printed on a large square of posterboard.

Adaptation for the Hearing Impaired.   Use sign language as appropriate.

Adaptation for the Visually Impaired.   Use bright, colorful objects with distinct shapes. Help your child use his hands and explore the size, shape, and arrangement of objects.

Adaptation for the Physically Impaired.   Give your child the necessary physical support so that he is successful. Decrease support as his skills improve. Consult your child's physical or occupational therapist if he has severe problems with muscle coordination and control, grasping, and releasing. The therapist may be able to individualize specific strategies for your child.

Chalkboard Games

These games will help your child to develop important eye-hand coordination and fine motor skills. These are the ingredients you'll need for this set of activities:

☆ Chalkboard and chalk
☆ Sponge
☆ Paintbrush
☆ Bowl of water

Here are a few Chalkboard games you can play with your child.

Balloon Pop Game

Draw a variety of different-sized balloons on the chalkboard. Explain to your child that he can pop the balloons by dipping the sponge in water and tracing over the balloons until they disappear. Remind him to trace over the lines of each balloon so he doesn't just wipe it away randomly. Once the chalkboard has dried, make more balloons. This time give your child a paintbrush to pop the balloons.

Chalkboard Drawings Game

Give your child and his brother or sister colored chalk. Suggest ideas for drawing, but give them time to create their own designs. Remember that scribbling is the first step in learning how to draw and write. Talk about what your child is making or scribbling, and encourage his attempts to control his lines and marks.

Dot-to-Dot Game

Make dot-to-dot drawings of houses, animals, flowers, or toys on the chalkboard using simple shapes of circles, squares, triangles, and rectangles. Give your child colored chalk to connect the dots and complete the line drawing. To make this game even more challenging, Mrs. Green numbers the dots for Johnny to follow.

Adaptation for the Visually Impaired.   Tape paper plates inside the balloons so your child can feel with his fingers and hands as he "pops" the balloons. For Dot-to-Dot, use flour paste (a thick, gooey mixture of flour and water) to make the dots. Let the dots dry so your child can feel them. Always use brightly colored chalk that contrasts strongly with the blackboard.

Adaptation for the Physically Impaired.   Consult your child's physical or occupational therapist for adaptive equipment and physical positioning to enhance your child's participation and performance. The suggestions listed for the visually impaired child are also helpful to your child as they provide additional physical prompts.

The Circle Game

This game is used to practice moving in different directions and associating directional words and meanings. Family and friends can join in this game.

Song: Melody—"Here We Go Loop De Loo, Here We Go Loop De Lie"

The circle goes round and round, the circle goes left, goes left, the circle goes right, goes right, all on a Saturday night. (The circle goes in, goes in, the circle goes out, goes out, up, down, etc.)

Join hands and practice walking in a circle. Sing the song while the circle moves in different directions.

Adaptation for the Hearing Impaired.   Use signs as needed.

The Popcorn Game

This game will help your child develop motor control and body awareness and will stimulate his imagination. These are the ingredients you'll need for this game:

☆ Cassette recorder and blank cassette

☆ Popcorn popper

☆ Popcorn and oil

☆ An old sheet

Everyone in the family sits around the sheet with the popcorn popper in the center. Your child can help pour the oil and popcorn into the popper and place the lid on it. As the popcorn pops, encourage everyone to watch as it "jumps," "tosses," and "explodes" and to listen carefully to the "crackling" sounds. Tape record the popcorn popping, from the very first pop until it has finished. Then explain that you are all going to pretend to be popcorn popping. Use the recorded tape to encourage different elements of movement, such as slow and fast movements corresponding to the popcorn sounds, quick bursts of energy, and changes of shape from little to big, and low to high. Repeat the tape several times to explore various ways of bursting in air and landing in a new shape. At the end of this activity, dig in and enjoy a snack! If you have a hot-air popper, try leaving the lid off to really see the pop-corn pop. Do not attempt this with an oil popper, as oil could splatter and burn someone.

SAFETY NOTE

To avoid injuries from hot kernels, do not allow children to be nearer than 3 feet to the popper.

Adaptation for the Physically Impaired.   For the child who has trouble getting both feet off the ground, try a modified jump with one foot leaving the ground at a time. Provide physical assistance when necessary. If the child is in a wheelchair, explore the various ways he can move his hands and arms.

Roly-Poly Games

The following games encourage rolling in different ways. These actions can be used in a game like Simon Says. Musical instruments or music from a record can be used for some of these activities.

Rolling Away and Rolling To Game

Everyone lies on the floor and rolls from one side of the room to the other. Roll toward the door, away from the window, or under the table. Remember to stop if you become dizzy. Try rolling over a variety of textures: soft, warm blanket; hard, cool floor; lumpy pillows, and a grassy area outside.

Musical Rolls Game

When the music starts, everyone rolls around the room together. When the music stops, all roly-polies stop, too.

Chain Roll Game

Lie end to end in a line, arms over head, holding hands or feet of another family member. Form a chain or divide into teams. Roll over and over as one unit.

If your child is unable to roll over by himself, use the techniques described in Rock 'n' Roll (page 54) to assist him. Brothers, sisters, and peers can be very helpful in motivating your child to play any kind of game. Describe to your child's siblings what you are trying to get your child to do and get them involved in playing with your child.

Adaptation for the Visually Impaired. For Roly-Poly games, use two different sound-making objects, such as a radio and a kitchen timer, and put them on opposite sides of the room to help give your child direction.

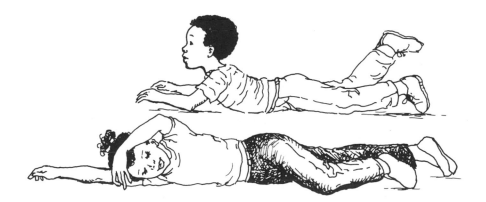

Adaptation for the Physically Impaired.   This activity should not be attempted without the supervision or guidance of a physical or occupational therapist.

Carpet Square Trail Games

Use these games to practice different motor and visual scanning skills and to improve understanding and recognition of spatial relationships. These are the ingredients you'll need for this set of activities:

☆ Carpet squares of different colors (carpet stores often give these away free or charge a nominal fee)

☆ Construction paper of different colors which match the carpet squares

☆ Musical record and record player

Here are a few Carpet Square Trail games you can play with your child.

Carpet Square Trail Leader Game

Make a carpet square trail for the family to follow. Play Follow the Leader; have the leader vary his actions as he moves from one square to another. Try walking, jumping, hopping, and skipping, or move from one square to another forwards, backwards, sideways, standing high, or squatting low.

Musical Carpet Squares Game

Play the Carpet Square Trail Leader game with music. Make sure everyone is a winner by having a carpet square for each person.

Rainbow Squares Game

Place different-colored carpet squares around a room or outside. Direct the child to walk from one color to another. If he has problems recognizing colors, hold up a piece of construction paper identical in color to the carpet square toward which you are directing him. Take turns with other family members in calling out directions. Place carpet squares "in front of," "next to," "behind," and "under" different pieces of furniture in the room. Take turns directing each other—"Go to the square under the table," or "Go to the square behind the couch."

Follow the Footsteps Games

These games will help your child to improve motor planning and coordination and will provide opportunities for visual tracking and directional orientation. These are the ingredients you'll need for this set of activities:

☆ Footprints (cut out of colored construction paper)

☆ Tape

☆ Large empty cardboard box

☆ Furniture and other large household objects

☆ Drum

☆ Record player and records

Here are two Follow the Footsteps games you can play with your child.

Through the Woods Game

Create "footsteps" inside the "woods" by arranging the paper footprints under the table, inside the cardboard box, around the chairs, and over furniture. Arrange the footsteps with consideration to your child's creeping, crawling, or walking pattern to ensure comfortable movement. Play Follow the Leader through the "woods" with all family members participating as hunters. This is a great opportunity to learn words and how to follow directions. Use words like "under," "through," and "around" as your child follows the footsteps.

Stop 'n' Go Game

Beat a drum or use a record player for this activity. When the music is playing, the hunters can move forward, stepping on the footprints. When the music stops, they must place their feet on a pair of footprints and stand still until the music begins again.

Adaptation for the Visually Imapaired.   Make the foorprints large and shiny or very brightly colored. If your child has very limited or no vision, he will need physical and verbal guidance. Use textured materials like sandpaper to make footprints, and let your child go barefoot.

Let's Play Ball Games

These games will encourage development of your child's large muscle control, eye-hand coordination, visual tracking, and basic ball-playing skills. They will also give the child a chance to play cooperatively with others. The games, organized in sequence from simple to more complex, will introduce your child to the give and take that is necessary to keep the game fun. Encourage the child's brother and/or sister to assist with these games. You'll need a lightweight ball (approximately 8 inches in diameter) to play. See individual games for additional ingredients.

Kick Mobile Game

Place your child on his back. Tie a lightweight ball, such as sponge ball, just above your child so he can reach it with his feet. Attach a small bell to the ball. Gently guide his foot to kick the ball, setting it in motion. Help him kick the ball until he catches on to this game and can do it by himself.

High Chair Toss Game

Place your baby in his high chair and help him to use both hands to hold a ball. Make sure the ball is large enough so he needs to use both hands to hold it. Help him hold the ball over the edge of the chair and release it so that it drops to the floor. Watch him to see if he looks for the ball once it has dropped out of sight. Ask him, "Where is your ball? Did you drop it?" Repeat until he catches on and can do it himself. Make sure he uses both hands and is not just pushing the ball over the edge. Use words such as "ball," "hold," "let go," and "over."

Ball Roll Game

Three people are needed to play this game. One family member sits behind your child. Another family member sits about 3 feet in front of the child and tells him, "Look, I have a ball." When you have the child's attention, tell him you are going to roll the ball to him. The family member behind the child can direct the child's attention to the ball and help him get his arms and hands ready to catch the ball. Give the child as much physical guidance as he needs. Roll the ball to the child. After he catches the ball, his helper can help him roll the ball back, if necessary. Play this game for as long as it holds your child's attention. Remember to give him lots of smiles and encouragement. This can also be done at a table with a child and partner sitting in chairs. Gradually decrease assistance so the child eventually rolls and catches the ball independently. Gradually add a soft bounce to this game and play with the child standing while you toss the ball from a squatting position. Practice bouncing and catching by showing your child how to drop the ball and catch it after a single bounce. Physically guide your child through the motions of using his arms and hands to catch the ball.

Tube Roll Game

Make a large tube out of posterboard. Sit next to your child on the floor. Roll a small ball to him through the tube. Tell him to put it back in and roll it to you. He will be delighted as he anticipates the ball coming out the end of the tube. This game helps your child to understand object permanence. Make sure to talk to him about what is happening when the ball is out of sight.

Roll Away Game

Use a slanted board. Show your child, or have a sister or brother show him, how to put the ball at the top of the board and let it roll down. He will have fun just watching the ball roll down and will learn to enjoy playing with balls. You can also place targets, such as milk cartons and shoe boxes, at the bottom of the ramp and aim the ball at them.

Tetherball Game

This game can be played in a standing or sitting position. Attach a lightweight ball or balloon to a rope or twine and hang it so that it is directly in front of your child at a level somewhere between his chest and eyes. Demonstrate to your child how to push or bat the ball with both hands. Just like in tetherball, push the ball back and forth to each other. To add more of a challenge to the game, use cardboard tubes from wrapping paper to bat the ball back and forth to each other.

Bowling Game

Set up a row of empty milk cartons, empty shoe boxes on end, or plastic bowling pins. Use two broomsticks for the alley (this will help guide the ball successfully toward the pins). You can also place a piece of flat cardboard on top of the row of "pins" and add a second row. Let your child bowl. Count how many objects he knocks over and how many are left. Let him help stack them back up. This game is fun for the whole family.

Stop and Go Game

Everyone stands in a circle. Pass the ball around the circle to music, with one family member controlling the record player. When the music stops, the person holding the ball has to stop. When the music starts again, continue to pass the ball around.

Basketball Game

Use an empty hamper, wastepaper basket, or cardboard box and a large ball or beanbag. Place the basket close to the child. Drop the ball into the basket. Let him try. Then move the basket farther away so he has to throw the ball to make a basket. Keep the basket close enough to your child to ensure his success. Move the basket to your child's far right and give him the beanbag in his left hand so he has to cross the middle of his body in order to drop or toss the beanbag in the target. Then move it to his left so his right arm crosses the middle of his body. Make sure he stays centered, whether he is standing or sitting, so that his arm reaches across the midline of his body.

Ball Bounce Game

Use an old sheet or lightweight blanket. Family members stand in a circle outside the perimeter of the sheet. Place a few foam balls, beach balls, or balloons on the sheet. All together, lift the sheet up and down and have fun watching the balls on the blanket. To play with two people, a brother or sister can be partners with your special child in this game, using a towel or small blanket. They will begin to understand that it takes both of them to keep the ball on the towel. The Greens love this game and play it outside with lots of balloons.

Mini-Kickball Game

Place your child in a low chair with a beach ball in front of him. Have your child kick the ball across the room to a family member who rolls it back. If your child has difficulty coordinating this effort, hold his ankle and swing his leg through the motion. Practice doing this until he is able to kick the ball independently while sitting in the chair.

Try playing Mini-Kickball in a standing position. If your child has trouble balancing, let him hold onto a family member or piece of furniture. Tell him to kick the ball to you. As he learns to balance himself, he will learn to kick the ball by walking into it with a shuffling motion. When your child masters kicking, place targets in front of him to knock over by kicking the ball into them.

Kickball Game

You will need construction paper or rug squares approximately 2 feet by 2 feet for bases, one ball, and two to three family members. Depending on your child's skills, decide whether to use one, two, or three bases. Starting with one base usually makes it easier to teach the basic rules of this game. Show your child where the first base is, then position him at home base with the ball in front of him. Tell him to kick the ball and run to first base. Have a family member at first base help him know where to run. After he runs to first, cheer and let him know that he is a great kickball player. Take turns with other family members and friends.

Adaptation for the Visually Impaired.   Use a "beep" ball (a ball that makes a *beep* sound), available through specialty retail outlets. Place a musical toy or kitchen timer in a target to help orient your child in terms of spatial relationships and directions.

Adaptation for the Physically Impaired.   Most of these games can be played by a child in a wheelchair or sitting down. If the child has limited or no use of his arms and hands, he can use his chin and forehead to push the ball. This is only for the child with strong head and neck control. If your child is in a wheelchair, try playing some of the games, such as bowling, at a table.

Jump 'n' Hop Games

These activities will help your child experience the movement and sensation of hopping (on one foot) and jumping (on two feet) as well as learn how to maintain balance while practicing specific motor skills.

These activities are for children who can stand and walk independently. These are the ingredients you'll need for this set of activities:

- ☆ Broomstick or thick roll of wrapping paper
- ☆ Thick rope
- ☆ Steps—bottom step of a stairway
- ☆ Phone books or sturdy, large wooden blocks
- ☆ 10 to 12 half-gallon milk cartons

Here are a few Jump 'n' Hop games you can play with your child.

Broomstick Hop Game

Hold a broomstick or roll of wrapping paper horizontally in front of your child at his chest level. Ask him to hold the center of the stick or roll, and place your hands on both sides of his. Explain that he will be hopping like a bunny. Use the broomstick or roll to help him balance as he hops up and down on both feet. While holding onto the broomstick or roll, both of you hop, one, two, three times. Have him try hopping on one foot. Maybe a brother or sister would like to try this one, too.

Rope Hop Game

Try Broomstick Hop using a rope. Hold it taut, about 12 inches across, so it gives the child the same feeling as the broomstick or roll. Gradually reduce the tension on the rope, thereby requiring the child to rely more on his own sense of balance.

One, Two, Three, Jump Game

Show your child that you can stand on a phone book or large building block and jump off. Place him on the phone book or block and

hold his hand while he practices jumping off. This may be very difficult for the child with perceptual-motor problems. Give him all
the support he needs to succeed at this activity. When he appears
comfortable jumping off the book or block, try having him jump
off the bottom step of a stairway.

Animal Jump Game

A brother or sister can play Animal Jump with your special child.
Pretend to be different animals (rabbit, kangaroo, frog, etc.) and
practice jumping like them to music. Bounce a ball and tell your
child to bounce up and down like the ball. Hold his hands while
you both bounce together. Encourage even his slightest attempt
to get both feet off the ground.

Over the Mountain Game

Place half-gallon milk cartons around the room in a circle. Use music with this game, preferably instrumental music with easily dis-
tinguishable slow and fast tempos. Each member of the family
stands behind a carton facing the same direction. When the music
begins, family members move around the circle and jump over the
milk cartons as they come to each one. When the tempo is slow,
everyone moves slowly; when the tempo is fast, they move faster.

When the music stops, everyone turns around and changes direction. Johnny likes this game so Mr. and Mrs. Green vary it by using hula hoops instead of milk cartons. They place the hula hoops flat on the floor in a circle around the room. As the family moves around the circle they must jump in and out of the hula hoops.

A commercially made "Hoppity-Hop" (a large, sturdy rubber ball with handles) makes for great fun and also helps the child work on balance and large muscle control. Using a Hoppity-Hop requires some of the same skills needed for hopping and jumping. Hoppity-Hop can be found at most children's toy stores.

Family Bunny Hop Game

This game will help your child develop independent hopping and balance skills. This activity is for children who can stand and walk independently. These are the ingredients and directions you'll need to play Family Bunny Hop:

- ☆ Red tape
- ☆ Yellow tape
- ☆ Colored construction paper and masking tape
- ☆ Record player
- ☆ Music record with tempos conducive to hopping

Cut out spots and tape them on the floor forming a circle. Space them so that it takes three child-sized hops to move from spot to spot. Place a patch of red tape or construction paper on each family member's right shoe and yellow on the left. Have each family member stand on a spot facing the same direction. Play a bunny hop song. When the bunnies hear you say "hop-hop-hop," they hop on one foot to the next spot, stopping when the music stops. Demonstrate this activity for your child before he attempts it. Explain that you will tell the bunnies which color foot to hop on ("yellow foot up" or "red foot up").

The Choo-Choo Express Game

This activity encourages motor planning, combining gross motor skills with the ability to sequence events. Play this in a large room or outside.

Use the following ingredients in any combination:

☆ Scooter board—to get from one station to another

☆ Toy train or bus—to move from station to station

☆ Card table—to crawl under

☆ Large blocks or carpet squares—to step on or jump over

☆ Large cardboard box—to crawl through, to push around

☆ Blanket—to drape over table, roll across, or crawl through

☆ Laundry basket—to step into

☆ Beanbags—to toss into the basket, to carry on your head

☆ Ladders—to walk across while ladder is flat on the floor, alternating feet or hopping with both feet together

☆ Picnic table benches—to crawl across

☆ Pillows—to walk on, throw, or hide under

☆ Low balance beam—to walk across forwards, sideways, or backwards

☆ Tires—to stand in or roll from one station to the next

☆ Hula hoop—to walk around, walk through, or jump into or out of

☆ Large sack or old pillowcase filled with foam rubber (such as those used for high jump field events)—lots of fun for jumping and falling on.

Mrs. Green sets up an obstacle course using any or all of the items on the ingredients list. Johnny goes from station to station by walking, crawling, hopping, riding a scooter board, or pushing a toy train. The first few times you do this activity with your child, demonstrate the activity first. Talk your way through the activity. Give him words to go with the actions. Your child might need you to go through the activity with him to remind him what to do. As your child goes through the activity, talk to him about what he is doing. Direct your child to try different actions to get from one station to the next. Refer to some of the other actions mentioned in this chapter (e.g., tiptoeing, crawling, hopping on one foot, jumping, walking very slowly, walking very fast, backwards or sideways walking, rolling).

Modify the game as you see fit. You might need to make the obstacle course shorter or add different obstacles to the course. Make sure everyone in the family takes turns. Always try to describe what is happening. While your child is awaiting his turn, ask him what his daddy or sister is doing at different points along the obstacle course. During his turn, ask him what he is doing at different stations. The Greens often set up the obstacle course in an area where it can be left for a few days and used again. This activity can include all the gross motor skills from creeping to hopping to walking backwards.

How to Make Scooter Boards

Scooter boards are fun, versatile toys that can be made at home. These instructions are for a long board (the exact length depends on your child's height) on which the child can lie on his stomach. If you don't feel like making a scooter board, you can order one from a commercial source. These are the ingredients you'll need to make a scooter board. The directions follow.

☆ A rectangle of 1/2-inch plywood—1.5 inches multiplied by the measurement of your child as described here

☆ Four ball-shaped casters with screws

☆ Rubber-backed carpet square or heavy fabric (3 inches larger on all sides than the top of the plywood)

☆ Foam rubber, 1 inch thick (cut to cover top of plywood)

☆ Staple gun

Measure your child from the armpit to 1 inch above the knee. Multiply this measurement by 1.5; cut the plywood to this length. Sand the board. Place foam rubber on top of the plywood. Cover foam rubber with fabric or carpet and wrap under plywood; using a staple gun, staple fabric or carpet to board. Attach casters with screws to each of the four corners of the scooter board.

Scooter-Mover Games

These games will help your child use both sides of his body to work together, integrate patterns of movement, and enhance motor planning skills, balance skills, and spatial awareness. These are the ingredients you'll need for this set of activities:

☆ Scooter board

☆ Hula hoop

☆ Milk cartons, shoe boxes, or oatmeal containers

☆ Beanbags

☆ Obstacle course

See specific activities for additional ingredients.

SAFETY NOTE

When your child rides the scooter board on his tummy, he should lift his legs and head up off the ground. Movement is achieved by paddling with the hands using alternating hand patterns. The same hand can be used if the child cannot alternate, but work toward alternating. Watch that little hands do not get caught under casters.

Here are a few more Scooter-Mover games you can play with your child:

Freestyle Take Off Game

Position and balance your child on his tummy on the scooter board. Allow your child to move about freely on the scooter board. Help him propel it by pushing off with his hands or feet.

Scooter Target Game

Place empty shoe boxes, milk cartons, and oatmeal containers 6 feet away from the wall, bowling-style. With your child on the scooter board on his tummy, show him how to push off the wall with his feet, his head toward the target, and knock over the target with his hands. Have your child try pushing off the wall with both hands, going backwards, so that he has to knock the target over with his feet.

Scooter Train Game

Family members line up on their scooter boards and form a train by holding onto each other's feet. Mom or Dad pulls the "engine," or first in line, with a hula hoop. Choo-choo goes the train! Johnny likes to be the engine and make the train sounds.

Beanbag Toss

Scatter beanbags or pint-sized milk cartons around the room. Place a box in the center of the room. Everyone paddles around the room picking up beanbags or milk cartons and tossing them into the box from a few feet away.

Red Light, Green Light Game

This is a fun game to play with scooter boards. Take turns being the light. Hold a red card and say, "Stop!" to mean stop. Hold a green card and say, "Go!" to mean go.

Scooter Course Game

Set up an obstacle course using chairs and boxes. Use some of the same ideas from the Obstacle Course activity, but use a scooter board. Your child, his brothers, and his sisters can take turns paddling forwards or backwards through the obstacle course.

Scooter Polo Game

Everyone crumples newspapers into balls. Each person paddles about on the scooter board and uses one or both hands to hold onto a cardboard tube and bat the ball to a target or another person. Try to keep elbows off the floor.

Scooter Pulley Game

Tie an 8- to 10-foot rope or bicycle inner tube between two stable 6-inch-high posts. Each person must move from one end to the other by pulling along the rope. Make this game into a simple relay race. Also, see chapter 7 for more relay races you can play on scooter boards.

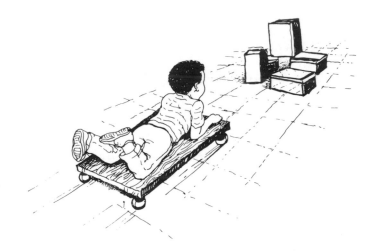

Match 'n' Adapt Playing Abilities

Although Johnny and his family enjoy these movement activities, feel free to create many more of your own. Even if your child has a physical impairment, you can help him get the movement experiences he needs by adapting the physical environment or the activities to match your child's abilities. Learn to break down difficult activities into simpler, easier steps. Always make sure that fun is the most important goal of any play activity. If it isn't fun, it's not play.

Chapter 4

EXPLORING THE WORLDS OF WATER PLAY, OUTDOORS, AND MAKE-BELIEVE

Imagine yourself at age 3 when everything was exciting and new. Remember sitting on the beach digging sand castles and waterways? No architect was wiser or more creative. Imagination and fantasy are wonderful for the developing child. Freedom of expression along with the proper resources gives the special child the opportunity to experience independence, creativity, and self-confidence.

The heart of play involves the child's world of imagination and make-believe. For this type of play allows the child to be director, producer and actor, viewing the world through her own eyes where everyday toys and objects are transformed into props for make-believe play.

The younger child will only be interested in discovering toys and objects in the most concrete sense. She will need to bang, drop, shake, taste, listen to, and examine the toys and objects you surround her with. As she begins to learn what toys are for she will roll the ball, push the car, and shake the tamborine. Later she may begin to elaborate by putting the doll to bed or pretending to drink out of toy cup.

Be alert to the first signs of fantasy or pretend play. If your child is physically impaired she may not be able to push the toy car "down the road" or "drink" out of the toy cup. You will need to physically assist her and, with her direction, set the stage for her.

Encourage pretend play by involving yourself. Choose toys that can be used in a variety of ways. Create opportunities to transform common household objects and toys into props and to explore the different ways they can be used. Freedom of expression with the proper resources will provide your child with the opportunities to experience independence, creativity, and self-confidence.

Outdoor play activities help children develop competence in motor skills and physical fitness and provide opportunities to learn about nature. This guide contains games for water play, sand fun, simple outdoor adventures, and arts and crafts. The games are adaptable to any situation or ability level. Encourage your child to express thoughts and feelings through these Splash 'n' Twirl, Outside World games. Here to guide you along is the Gold Family.

The Gold Family Plays Splash 'n' Twirl, Outside World Games

Sarah Gold is a lively 5-year-old with Down Syndrome. She was adopted by Mr. and Mrs. Gold, a couple in their late 40s, 2 years ago. She is a happy, robust little girl who likes to play and explore with her parents. Her parents are eager to encourage family fun.

Soap Bubble Fun Games

These games will encourage your child to visually track and reach for the bubbles she sees. It is a good way to practice breath control, which is important in developing good speech habits. These are the ingredients you'll need for this set of activities:

☆ 1/4 cup liquid dishwashing detergent
☆ 1 cup water
☆ A few drops of food coloring
☆ 1 teaspoon sugar
☆ Small plastic squeeze bottle or squirt gun
☆ Pipe cleaners or bubble wand

Here are two Soap Bubble Fun games you can play with your child.

Bubble Blow Game

Combine the first four ingredients to make the bubble solution. Shape a pipe cleaner into a circle at one end and loop tightly. Dip the pipe cleaner or bubble wand into the mixture and blow lots of big bubbles.

Pop Goes the Bubble Game

One child or adult blows bubbles and the others try to catch them before they land on the ground. Vary the game by using different body parts to pop the bubbles. For example, step on the bubble, clap the bubble, kick the bubble, or use the squeeze bottle or squirt gun to pop the bubble. Have fun just chasing and catching the bubbles.

> **SAFETY NOTE**
>
> Before using this or any other bubble liquid, make sure your child is not allergic to the ingredients. Closely supervise children who might try to drink the bubble mixture. Keep the bubble mixture away from eyes.

Water Play Games

These activities will help to develop important motor skills as well as stimulate creative fun and play. These are the ingredients you'll need for this set of activities:

☆ Child's outdoor pool or vinyl infant bathtub

☆ Plastic containers of several different sizes and shapes

☆ Squeeze bottles, funnel, strainer, windmill, squirt guns, sponges, spray bottle, measuring spoons

☆ Ice cubes

☆ Styrofoam squares

☆ Paper

☆ Toothpicks

☆ Plastic straws

Here are a few Water Play games you can play with your child.

Water Play Fun Game

It's hot out. Put on your bathing suits and let the family enjoy the wonders of water. Create and play games using a shallow plastic pool of water and a variety of unbreakable kitchen containers and utensils. Demonstrate pouring from container to container. Try using a funnel, a cooking baster, a strainer, or measuring spoons. Place the very young child on your lap and help her to enjoy moving, splashing, and feeling comfortable in the water.

Icebergs Game

On a hot day it's always fun to add a tray or two of ice cubes to the water. It gives the child an opportunity to see ice float and to feel temperature extremes.

Target Squirt Game

Give each child empty squeeze and squirt containers or a water gun. Show your child how to fill and squirt. It's fun to squirt at a cloth target that will look wet when you hit it or at a target that makes noises, such as aluminum foil, a metal cookie sheet, or a plastic surface. Noise-making targets are essential for the visually impaired child.

Boat Float Game

How about a boat race? Mr. Gold and Sarah make their own sail-boats, using a piece of paper as the sail, a square of styrofoam as the base, and a toothpick as the mast. They race their sailboats using straws to blow the boats across the water in Sarah's inflatable wading pool.

Bathtub Fun Game

All these games can be played year-round in a bathtub, sink, washtub, or large bucket.

Adaptation for Children in Wheelchairs or Other Special Seating. Place a tub of water on a table and seat the child at the table.

Bath 'n' Splash Games

These activities will promote appreciation of the joy of water play and develop preswimming skills, while further developing other important motor and social skills. These are the ingredients you'll need for this set of activities:

- ☆ Bathtub, small children's pool, or full-sized swimming pool
- ☆ Toys that sink and float, ping-pong balls, balloons
- ☆ Bubble bath (make sure your child is not allergic to its ingredients)

Here are a few Bath 'n' Splash games you can play with your child.

Squeak Bath 'n' Splash Game

Introduce your child to water during bathtime. Begin the bath with a bit of splashing and allow your child to get used to being surrounded by water. Put a floating squeak toy or plastic boat in the tub and let your child make it "swim" around her as she swishes the water, pulling with one hand and pushing with the other. Show her how to change the direction in which the toy travels by reversing the movement of her hands and arms. Float a small plastic bowl in the tub and encourage your child to use it as a steering wheel to sail her boat. Use containers, funnels, and colanders in the tub for pouring. Show your child how to scoop up water in one container and pour it into another. Show her how to squeeze a sponge so the water trickles on her tummy, through her hands, on her knees and toes. Squeezing will also help to build important strength in fingers and hands.

Many children find putting their faces in the water frightening. Do not force your child to put her face in the water; this will only make it more uncomfortable for her. Begin by having her place just her forehead in the water. Demonstrate, or have a brother or sister demonstrate. Make this a game by asking your child how much of her face can touch the water. Show her how to draw circles in the water with her nose, chin, or forehead. Help her explore the different ways she can move her arms and legs in the bathtub. Hide a toy or various body parts under bubbles during a bubble bath.

Blowing Bubbles Game

Once your child is comfortable getting her face wet, you can teach her how to blow bubbles. Many children have difficulty understanding the difference between breathing in, breathing out, and holding their breath. Make this a game by demonstrating blowing bubbles under water for your child. Saying sounds, talking, or singing will help her automatically blow out when she is under water. Other activities can include these:

- Making a hole in the water by blowing into it above the surface
- Blowing across the surface of the water to make a wave
- Blowing ping-pong balls or balloons across the water to a playmate
- Saying your name or another word under water
- Placing a mirror at the bottom of a bowl of tepid water to encourage blowing bubbles and opening eyes under water
- Pretending there is a birthday cake with candles under the water and blowing out the candles
- At the swimming pool, have the whole family hold hands, form a circle, and go under the water together. Play Ring Around the Rosy, and scream or make silly sounds under the water.

Small Folk Pool Fun Games

Move out of the tub and into the pool by beginning in the children's pool or the shallow end of a regular pool. Use the same games you played in the bathtub to introduce your child to the pool. In the beginning, use inflatable arm bands or doughnut rings so your child will stay afloat. Encourage her to splash with her hands and arms. Play getting-the-face-wet games as you did in the bathtub. Ask your child to try moving her body various ways in the water: arms spread out and up high, standing on one leg (with your assistance if necessary), jumping like a kangaroo. Practice blowing bubbles using the suggestions listed in the activity at the start of the chapter.

Many of the singing and circle games found in chapter 6, "Rap 'n' Rhyme, Music Time," are great fun when played in the water. Now that Sarah can hold her breath and blow bubbles under the water, she and Mr. and Mrs. Gold play Ring Around the Rosy or Humpty Dumpty at the pool. They bring various toys that sink and float to the pool and help Sarah retrieve a toy that has sunk to the bottom. This encourages her to keep her eyes open under the water and to hold her breath. To retrieve a floating toy Sarah lies on her tummy with her body extended outward. Mr. Gold supports Sarah, placing his hands under her trunk or chest, and pulls her toward the floating object, encouraging her to grab it with her hand. Sarah kicks and makes big splashes to move toward the floating toy. This is an important preswimming activity.

SAFETY NOTE

Never swim at a pool without a competent lifeguard, and never leave your child alone—not even for one second!

Washing Games

These activities will help to develop representational play skills. It is important for a child to feel like a special helper around the house with Mom and Dad. These are the ingredients you'll need for this set of activities:

☆ Child's tricycle or any type of toy car

☆ Bucket, sponge, water, liquid dishwashing detergent

☆ Towels

☆ Washable dolls

Here are two Washing games you can play with your child.

Family Car Wash Game

When washing the family car, fill a plastic bucket with water, add some suds, and make it a family project. Help your child wash her bike or wagon as you wash the car. Let her help wash the car too. Remember, cleaning up together is also part of the game.

Wash 'n' Dry Game

Fill a bucket or plastic bathtub with water and get ready to wash a baby doll. This is a great deal of fun and can be a cooperative effort between your special child and her sister or brother. Make sure to wash the different body parts (arms, legs, hands, feet, etc.) and talk about what your child is doing. Take turns by having one child wash the baby and another dry. This is also a good game to play in the bathtub.

Backyard Water Slide Game

This activity will give your child a delightful sensory-motor experience. These are the ingredients you'll need for this activity:

- ☆ Old plastic or vinyl shower curtain
- ☆ Plastic jugs filled with water
- ☆ Water hose
- ☆ Liquid detergent (optional)

Here is a Backyard Water Slide game you can play with your child.

Mrs. Gold spreads an old shower curtain on a hill in the yard. She uses plastic jugs filled with water to hold down the corners, then sprays the curtain with water so it is completely wet. She puts a few drops of liquid detergent on the plastic to add to the slipperiness—then the fun begins. Sarah loves to sit on the curtain and enjoy the slide down the hill.

SAFETY NOTE

Supervise children closely—wet plastic is very slippery! Don't forget to check for rocks or sharp objects on the ground before putting down your curtain.

Adaptation for the Physically Impaired.   If your child can't sit or stand well enough to do this activity, try a position that she can manage. Lay your child on her tummy with arms outstretched and pull her along the slippery slide. This is a wonderful movement and

sensory experience. You can also hold your child on your lap and slide down the hill together.

House and Sidewalk Painting Games

These activities will enhance your child's motor skills, eye-hand coordination, and creative play skills. These are the ingredients you'll need for this set of activities:

- ☆ Bucket filled with water
- ☆ Large and small paintbrushes
- ☆ Painter's cap (optional)
- ☆ Paint rollers and tray
- ☆ Chalk
- ☆ Several containers of food coloring
- ☆ Plastic containers or paper cups
- ☆ Tempera paint

Here are a few House and Sidewalk Painting games you can play with your child.

House Painting Game

Sarah enjoys pretending to be a housepainter. She puts on a cap and a pair of old overalls, and Mr. Gold gives her a paintbrush and a bucket filled with water. She paints the outside of the house, a tree, or a fence. It's always more fun to "paint" when a child can see what she has painted. Surfaces that darken when wet are best.

Sidewalk Designs Game

Paint designs, write names, or outline body parts (hands, feet, or the whole body) with colored chalk, tempera paint or food coloring on a concrete sidewalk or driveway. Have your child step in a bucket of water and then walk on the sidewalk, making footprints. Have everyone in the family join in on this one and then compare small, medium, and big feet.

Balloon Pop Game

Draw pictures of balloons on the sidewalk with chalk or tempera paint. To "pop" the balloons, paint over them with a wet paintbrush and water.

SAFETY NOTE

Have your child wear long pants and give her a rubber door mat or carpet square to sit on so she does not scrape or bruise herself on the cement.

Sand Play Games

These activities will enhance fine motor skills, eye-hand coordination, and creative play skills. These are the ingredients you'll need for this set of activities:

☆ Large empty cardboard box, old tire, or wading pool

☆ Sand (white construction sand is preferable because it does not stain clothing) or a substitute (cornmeal, oatmeal, Styrofoam packing material)

☆ Cans of all sizes, milk cartons, spoons, paper cups, buckets, molds, shovels, watering cans, funnels, ice cube trays, any other types of plastic containers

☆ Plastic animals and people, sturdy cars and trucks

Here are a few Sand Play games you can play with your child.

Making a Sand Box

If you do not already have a sandbox, here's how to make a quick and easy one. Fill a large, shallow cardboard box or an old tire with sand. Children can kneel beside their sandbox or tire, sit in it, or stand in it. Have several of the household items mentioned above available for creative play. Children will enjoy filling the containers with sand and pouring it out. Encourage them to create roadways and houses and to make pretend cookies or meatballs. Bury toys or even a hand under the sand. Play hide and find games with toys. There are endless opportunities for fun in the sand.

Sand Sculptures Game

Pack wet sand into plastic containers of different sizes and shapes. Create sand castles, houses, and cities.

Sand Designs Game

Place some sand across a large surface, add water, and draw designs with fingers and sticks. Make sure the surface is smooth before designing.

Adaptation for the Physically Impaired.   Physically guide and assist your child as needed. If your child has difficulty grasping and manipulating objects with her hands and fingers, place a Velcro mitten or band on her hand or arm. Affix another piece of Velcro to the sandbox toys.

Rumble Tumble Games

These activities will help to develop motor skills and motor planning through outdoor sensory experiences. These are the ingredients you'll need for this set of activities:

　☆ Target objects such as empty milk cartons, or shoe boxes
　☆ Leaves and a rake

Here are two Rumble Tumble games you can play with your child.

Target Roll Game

Children love to roll down hills. Most adults do too. Here's your chance to relive your childhood. Place target objects on the hill or at the bottom, bowling-pin style. Try to knock them down with your body as you roll down the hill.

Leaf Crunch Game

Rake some leaves together and have fun sitting, moving, rolling, and jumping into the pile of leaves and crunching them.

Adaptation for the Physically Impaired.   Your child can roll a ball down the hill in order to knock over the target objects.

Outdoor Art Activities

These activities will provide your child with enjoyable fine motor, gross motor, and creative play opportunities. These are the ingredients you'll need for this set of activities:

- ☆ Large sheets of construction paper, butcher paper, or newsprint
- ☆ Paintbrush
- ☆ Fingerpaint or liquid tempera paint
- ☆ Outside area

Here are two Outdoor Art games you can play with your child.

Footprint Mural Game

Place paper on the ground outside. Paint the bottom of your child's feet. If your child cannot tolerate the feeling of the brush, spread the paint on a paper plate or in a cake pan and let her step in the paint. Then let her walk delightedly across the paper, leaving colorful footprints. Wash her feet off and apply a different color, or, better yet, have each member of the family walk across the paper, each making a different color footprint.

Outdoor Painting Fun

Painting and craft activities are more fun when done outdoors, and cleanup is easier—just use the hose. Try finger painting, brush painting, body painting, or any of the activities from chapter 5.

Up, Up, and Away Games

These activities will enhance your child's motor, visual, tracking, and scanning skills. These are the ingredients you'll need for this set of activities:

- ☆ Lots of balloons or sponge balls
- ☆ Construction paper
- ☆ Kite string
- ☆ Fabric squares
- ☆ Fishing weight
- ☆ Parachute or an old sheet
- ☆ String
- ☆ Paper clasp or clip
- ☆ Unsharpened pencil or eraser

Here are a few Up, Up, and Away games you can play with your child.

Balloon Up, Up, and Away Game

Blow up balloons and let them go without tying them. Have your family chase after the balloons as they fly around losing air. Suggest that they act out the balloon's movement as it goes up and comes down.

Parachute Launch Game

Space family members and friends evenly around a parachute or sheet. Place many inflated balloons or sponge balls on the parachute. Lift and lower the parachute. See how long you can keep the objects on the parachute or how fast you can get them off.

Making a Parachute

Help your child make a parachute. Tie a string to each corner of a handkerchief-sized square of fabric. Tie the loose ends of the string to a single heavy object, such as a small fishing weight. Show your child how to toss the parachute up in the air so that it unfolds and drifts to the ground.

Paper Airplanes Game

Fold paper to simulate an airplane; show your child how to fly the aircraft.

Pinwheel Fun Game

Make a simple pinwheel. Take a square of sturdy construction paper and cut from each corner toward the center, leaving at least 1 inch uncut. Place every other cut point in the center and secure with a paper clasp. Stick the paper clasp into the eraser end of a pencil, which serves as a handle. Blow the pinwheel and show your child how it works. On a windy day, let the wind do the work for you.

Making a Kite

These are the ingredients you'll need to make a kite.

- ☆ Two 3/16-inch by 24-inch dowel rods
- ☆ Covering material, at least 24 inches by 30 inches (a large plastic garbage can liner works well)
- ☆ Cellophane tape
- ☆ Filament strapping tape
- ☆ Line for bridle and for flying
- ☆ Scissors
- ☆ Hole punch
- ☆ Markers or paints

Cut the covering material into the shape of the kite. Tape on the two dowel rods, using four or five pieces of cellophane tape for each dowel. Reinforce the corners for the bridle with strapping tape. Use two pieces on each corner, one piece on each side of the material (i.e., sandwich the material with the tape). Trim the tape to conform to the edge of the kite and punch a hole in each corner. Take a piece of line about 6 feet long and tie one end into each hole you've punched. Make sure the knots don't slip. Find the midpoint in the bridle that you've just attached, and tie a small loop there. This loop is where you will attach the flying line. If the kite pitches to one side while flying, you may not have centered the loop and you will have to retie it. Decorate the kite. Use large designs and thick lines. Fill the whole space between the dowels. Tie on the flying line. The kite flies with the dowels (and design) toward the ground and the flier. The best way to launch the kite is not to run with it, but to have one person hold the kite, facing the flier, while the flier takes the line and stands about 20 yards away. The flier quickly pulls in a few handfuls of line while the helper releases the kite. Have fun!

Adaptation for the Physically Impaired.   Your child can enjoy all of the Up, Up, and Away Games even if she is physically unable to handle the parachute, aircraft, or balloons. As long as she can see, she'll have fun just watching. Be sure to talk about what is happening.

Shadow Games

These games will help develop imitation skills and creative imagination. These are the ingredients you'll need for this set of activities:

☆ Flashlight

☆ Bright sunny day and a sidewalk

Here are a few Shadow Games you can play with your child.

Wall Show Game

Direct a flashlight or film projector toward a plain white wall. Everyone in the family can experiment with free-form hand and body movements, just having fun with their own shadows. Try different improvisations: Be a flower growing, a tree blowing in the wind, a bird flying, an airplane taking off, a bunny rabbit hopping, a basketball player, a ballet dancer, or just a regular person doing regular things. Use favorite puppets for a puppet shadow show.

Shadow Images Game

Help your child to pair up with another member of the family. One person performs a basic body movement and the other person creates a "shadow" by imitating her partner. Take turns being the leader and the follower.

Walking Shadows Game

Take a walk outside on a bright sunny day. Jump onto each other's shadows and say "Gotcha!" Or try some of the ideas from the Wall Show game while you are outside.

Family Story Time Games

These activities will help your child begin to enjoy and appreciate books. They will also help her to understand that familiar and important parts of her world can be represented by pictures. These are the ingredients you'll need for this set of activities:

- ☆ Recent photographs of your family members
- ☆ Pictures from magazines
- ☆ Old, torn storybooks or nursery rhyme books
- ☆ Heavy construction paper or posterboard cut into squares with holes punched out for binding
- ☆ Yarn to bind book
- ☆ Clear contact paper to protect pages of the picture books
- ☆ Popsicle sticks

Here are a few Family Story Time games you can play with your child.

Storybook Fun Game

Start early in your child's life with books that have large simple pictures with only one picture to a page. Look at the pictures together, pointing to them and identifying them one at a time. Your child will be able to point to pictures and understand what you are saying long before she is able to name the pictures herself. As your child grows and develops, so will the stories you share. As her attention span and language develop, select favorite stories from your own childhood as well as new books. Schedule special times for looking at pictures, reading a storybook together, or just using your own simple sentences to tell a story. Involve your child by asking her to point to certain pictures or asking her questions as her vocabulary and language ability increase. Eventually involve her imagination to add to the fun.

My Family Book Game

The Golds enjoyed making a book with photographs of their family. They included Sarah's grandparents, aunts and uncles, and

other familiar and important people. They put only one picture on each page, one person to a picture, and printed the person's name beneath the picture. They often look at the pictures with Sarah, identifying each picture and telling her something about the person. Sarah likes to pat, touch, or point to the pictures as Mr. and Mrs. Gold talk about them.

My Favorite Activities Book Game

Make a book using magazine pictures of your child's favorite things. Cut out pictures of her favorite toys, activities, food, clothes, and other pictures that may be interesting to her. You can also use photographs of your child playing. Help your child decorate the front of the book. Encourage her to tell you about each picture, and add short, simple captions from her ideas and thoughts. Other family members can share in the fun by taking time to look through her special book with her.

Family Story Game

Cut out and paste photographs of family members on popsicle sticks to make puppets. Begin by telling a short, simple story about your family with the puppets. Encourage your child and her brothers and sisters to add to and tell part of the story. Use stories of special times, traditional family celebrations, and day-to-day activities and routines. Encourage your child's participation by asking questions: "What happened next?" "What do you think the person did then?" "How did it make him (her) feel?" Use these puppets, or puppets with pictures of people from magazines, to make up imaginary stories. You might be surprised to see how closely these stories relate to you child's perception of her own world and the people who are an important part of it.

Puzzle Stories Game

Cut out a series of three to five pictures from an old storybook or nursery rhyme book. Place the pictures in sequence and tell your child a short version of a familiar story. Mix the pictures up and encourage your child to place the pictures back in the right order and tell the story in her words. Increase the number of pictures depending on your child's ability level. For a variation of this activity, use pictures that are not associated and create your own stories. This can be lots of fun for the whole family.

Adaptation for the Hearing Impaired. Use sign language as needed.

Adaptation for the Visually Impaired. Use lots of verbal descriptions when telling or making up stories.

Let's Pretend Games

These activities will help your child begin representational and symbolic play, which is an important ingredient for more sophisticated dramatic and imaginative play. Dolls are valuable for both boys and girls. These are the ingredients you'll need for this set of activities:

☆ Dolls, teddy bears, and puppets

☆ Brush

☆ Bottle

☆ Plastic cups, bowls, and silverware

☆ Doll blanket or bed

☆ Doll carriage

☆ Miniature dolls, plastic people, animals, toy trucks and cars

☆ Doll house, toy barn with animals, garage, or village

☆ Household props such as pots, pans, or broom

Here are two Let's Pretend games you can play with your child.

Doll Play Game

Set the stage in a very simple way for your child, boy or girl, to begin the first steps toward imaginative play. Demonstrate to your child how to pretend to drink out of an empty cup or eat from an empty spoon. Don't forget the appropriate sound effects. Your child will have fun imitating your "Mmmm, so good." Pretend to go to sleep. Use your child's favorite doll and a bottle or cup, plastic bowl, and spoon. Say to your child, "Doll baby is so hungry. Can you feed him?" Help your child use two objects together, such as the spoon and the bowl, to feed the doll. After the doll is fed, which may take only a few seconds as dolls eat quickly, say, "Doll baby is so sleepy. Should we put him in bed?" Get the doll ready for bed. Cover the doll with a blanket. Brush the doll's hair or get the doll ready for a bath. When your child is engaged in playing with the doll, be sure to describe what she is doing. Your own enthusiasm will help to capture your child's attention. Always expand on this type of play by picking up on and imitating what your child is doing. Help your child act out her own daily routine during doll play.

House Play Game

Set the scene by using a variety of real-life props or toys that closely resemble household objects, such as a toy vacuum cleaner. Encourage your child to pretend to be the mommy, daddy, or baby with pretend play that represents daily experiences in your home. Pretend play may be very brief and isolated without adherence to the true sequence of events. This will come when your child is older. To enhance this type of play further, use the miniature props listed in the ingredients. Help your child use miniature dolls and other props to play house, shopping, school, and other important activities in her life. Your child's developmental level in all areas (large and small motor, verbal, intellectual, social) will determine her level of imaginary play. As your child's abilities develop, try following her lead rather than directing her play.

Adaptation for the Physically Impaired. Give your child physical assistance as needed so that she can be as physically involved as possible with the activity. Use larger toys or dolls rather than miniature ones. If your child has difficulty grasping objects, use a Velcro mitten, glove, or band fitted to hand, head, or foot. Affix the other side of the Velcro to the doll, car, or other objects. If your child has a severe language impairment, use a communication display with pictures of toys and activities which can be acted out on the board, or follow your child's directions with real-life objects.

Box Creation Games

These activities will help to develop imagination and creative play skills. These are the ingredients you'll need for this set of activities:

- ☆ Cardboard boxes of assorted sizes
- ☆ Large empty cardboard appliance boxes
- ☆ Old sheet, blanket, or towel
- ☆ Construction paper
- ☆ Crayons, markers, paint, paintbrushes, yarn, liquid glue, foam packing beads, and any other decorative material
- ☆ Flashlight
- ☆ Store props: pretend food, toy cash register, toy dishes and cups
- ☆ Dress-up clothes

Here are a few Box Creation games you can play with your child.

Towers Game

Different-sized cardboard boxes make large towers for stacking and knocking down.

Play House Game

Mrs. Gold got a large cardboard refrigerator shipping carton from an appliance store. She helped Sarah decorate it with tempera paint. Then she cut out a door and windows. Sarah likes to pretend it is a house, a school, or a tepee. Mrs. Gold gave Sarah some milk cartons, paper bags, and yarn to glue onto the box. She decorated windows with curtains made from old sheets (you could also use dish towels or fabric remnants). Sarah likes to use a flashlight to provide light in her hideaway.

Dress-Up Game

An all-time favorite—fill a box with old shirts, dresses, hats, shoes, jewelry, scarves, and other accessories that you no longer need. Hats can be transformed into crowns, nurse's caps, or cowboy hats. If your child has few ideas to start with, you and a brother or sister can inspire her by joining in the dress-up fun and pretend play. Try to relate your child's recent experiences, such as a birthday party or something that happened at school, to her play.

Food Store Game

Once the Play House is built, turn it into a grocery store or your child's favorite fast-food restaurant. This will encourage your child's imagination and open the doors for pretend play. With the help and friendly encouragement of a brother or sister, the decorated box becomes a place to buy and eat food. Cut food out of construction paper or use plastic models. Use pretend money for purchasing groceries or paying for a hamburger, french fries, and a shake.

Going on a Trip Game

Line up several boxes, like those you can get from the grocery store, in a row, or use a large, empty appliance box with cut-out windows to create a family or neighborhood bus. Each person can specially design his or her own seat, using the suggestions from the Play House activity. Once everyone is sitting down on the bus, sing and pretend to go on a trip and, depending on where you are going, talk about what the children need to pack. Ask the children to think of other vehicles that the boxes could be, such as airplanes, boats, cars, trucks, fire engines, and trains.

Dramatic Play Games

This play activity will help your child to further develop creative and imaginative play skills. Do not limit your child's choices because of gender roles. You will need props for a specific situation or role that is familiar to your child. Suggestions follow.

- Doctor or nurse: Nurse's cap, medical play kit, tape, gauze, cotton, bandages, ace bandage, smock (for doctor or nurse's coat), bed or cot
- Ice cream store owner: Empty ice cream containers, ice cream scoop, cap and apron, play cash register and play money, cones made from construction paper, ice cream made of colored balls or pom-poms to fit on top of cones
- Dress-up: Mom's or Dad's old clothes and accessories
- Firefighter: Pieces of old garden hose, raincoats, boots, play firefighter hat, a big empty box to transform into fire truck
- Office worker: Typewriter, telephone, paper, pencil
- Farmer: Pieces of Styrofoam to be seeds to plant, hose to water plants, plastic flowers, plants, foods to grow and pick
- Airline pilot: Old hat for pilot's hat, empty box for an airplane, paper plate for steering wheel
- Grocery clerk: Toy cash register, grocery bags, apron, empty cans and boxes of food to purchase, box or wagon as basket to carry food, play money
- Use one of the suggested themes or one of your child's own ideas, and provide the necessary props. Encourage your children and her friends to create their own dramatic play themes. Dramatic play can be one of the most effective forms of communication for children. If your child has difficulty with this type of play, help her set the scene by playing with her and asking questions to direct her imagination. This can be a group or individual activity.

Nature Creation Activities

See individual activities for ingredients for these activities.

Leaf People Activity

(Ingredients: Paper, liquid glue, leaves) Collect leaves and make leaf people or any other interesting designs on paper.

Nature Rubbing Activity

(Ingredients: Crayons, drawing paper) Place paper on an object or part of an object. Examples include a telephone pole, a fire hydrant, a tree trunk, leaves, a sidewalk, or a grassy area. Rub a crayon over the paper so the object's texture becomes visible. Collect several rubbings and take turns guessing the objects. For young children, tape or hold the paper on the object. Make a collage of different patterns and colors from the rubbings.

Rock Garden Activity

(Ingredients: Shoe box top, dirt, rocks, pebbles, twigs, moss, grass, small mirror, and miniature animals, people, vehicles, and buildings) Mrs. Gold puts a thin layer of dirt into the top of a shoe box. Sarah uses the small mirror as a reflecting pool and places different types of moss at the edge of the pool. Twigs stuck between clumps of moss form trees. She adds a rock and some pebbles near the water's edge. She puts more twigs, moss, grass, and rocks into this little garden and adds animals, vehicles, people, and buildings from her toy box. Sarah loves to change the position of animals and people as she creates stories to go with the scene. To make a winter scene, use cotton or soap flakes for snow.

Adaptation for the Physically Impaired.   Give your child physical assistance as needed. Use adaptive material such as a Velcro mitten or band on your child's hand. Attach the other side of the Velcro to objects used. Use larger objects that are easier to grasp. If this activity is too difficult for your child, let her direct you in making a rock garden.

Treasure Hunt Games

These activities will give your child opportunities to solve problems and develop language. These are the ingredients you'll need for this set of activities:

☆ Large bag of peanuts in their shells
☆ Small containers or cups
☆ Color-coded prizes
☆ Treasure clues
☆ Hat or box
☆ Picture list

Here are a few Treasure Hunt games you can play with your child.

Backyard Treasure Hunt Game

Select an open area in your backyard or in a neighborhood park for a peanut hunt. Hide peanuts where they can be found easily. Give each child a small container or paper or plastic cup to collect peanuts. Allow enough time for all participants to gather as many peanuts as they can. Once all the peanuts are found, eat and enjoy them! For older children, try this game with pennies.

SAFETY NOTE

Do not use peanuts if your child is under age 3 or has difficulty swallowing.

Color Hunt Game

Wrap small prizes in different-colored paper or place in bags tied with colored ribbon or yarn. Assign a different color to each player or team. Give each child a bag marked with her color and tell her to find all the prizes that match the color on her bag. This is a great birthday party game.

Prize Hunt Game

Hide prizes in the backyard or park. Prepare picture clues to the location of various prizes. Examples include pictures of the swing set, a bird feeder, a large oak tree, or other items found in an outside area. Children select their treasure clues out of a hat or box and hunt for their treasure. At the end of the hunt, each child finds a special prize. This game can be played by one or many children, individually or in teams.

Scavenger Hunt Game

Give each child or family member a written or picture list of five or six items that can be found outdoors, such as a leaf, rock, clover, or stick. Have a race to see who can be first to find all of the items on the list. This is a good game to play in teams.

Detective Walk Games

These activities will provide your child with important language, observation, and problem-solving experiences. As you play these games, teach children to think before they take and not to collect things that should remain for all people to enjoy. These are the ingredients you'll need for this set of activities:

- ☆ Cardboard tubes from paper towels or toilet paper
- ☆ Snacks—fruit, nuts, cheese, popcorn (for hungry detectives)
- ☆ Backyard or neighborhood park
- ☆ Bucket, empty shoe box, or paper bag

Here are a few Detective Walk games you can play with your child.

Detective Scope Walk Game

Use tubes as telescopes or microscopes to explore different objects in nature; or just explore without the tubes. Give each detective a bucket, empty shoe box, or paper bag. Look for and collect leaves, acorns, sticks, rocks, flowers, weeds, ferns, and other outdoor objects of various sizes, shapes, and colors. Assign your detectives to find

- The biggest/smallest leaf
- The bumpiest thing they can
- The softest thing
- The smoothest rock
- The roughest stick
- Something that is beautiful

Feely Box Game

Collect a bag full of nature objects, bring them home, and make a Feely Box. Sort stones, leaves, or other objects by color, size, or shape. Blindfold your child and encourage her to identify objects by touch.

Safari Hunt Game

A group leader collects various outdoor objects mentioned in Detective Scope Walk. The leader holds up one object at a time and gives a signal for each hunter to find the same. This is a great opportunity to match an older brother or sister with your special child. Make a safari mural when all the objects have been collected.

Detective Tracks Game

Cover the bottom of a plastic dishpan or other container with damp sand. Collect a variety of small objects from outdoors as well as familiar household objects such as a comb, fork, cookie cutter, pencil, and toy car. Ask your child to close her eyes while you make tracks in the sand with one of the objects. Ask your child to look at the tracks and tell you, point to, or give you the object she thinks was used to make the tracks. Help your child describe how the tracks look in terms of size and shape. Take turns playing this game with the whole family.

Discover Other Playtime Resources

Playing in the water and sand, enjoying nature and outdoor activities, and exploring the delights of make-believe and imaginative play are important to every child's development. The activities described in this chapter are only a few suggestions for you and your child. You can also find many good ideas in books available at your local library. Don't forget that your child's teachers or therapists can be wonderful sources as well.

Chapter 5

EXPLORING THE WORLD OF ARTS AND CRAFTS

In your eyes, the first flower you drew was a masterpiece. Your first portrait, a study in creativity. Art allows a freedom of expression and creativity not found in most other play activities. Through art, the disabled child can learn and explore in a less structured way than with toys and games. Every part of the body—arms, hands, legs—can become a paintbrush, every part of the day a chance to create.

The young artist is less concerned with the final product than with the fun involved in creating something. Because beauty is in the eye of the beholder, arts and crafts are foolproof. No matter what the final product, every artist sees his creation as unique and beautiful, simply because he did it! Have fun with these art activities. Create an atmosphere that stimulates your child to explore, experiment, and feel positive about his efforts. When your child explores an idea in a unique way, encourage him, even though he may not be following the process you had in mind.

Explore the world of art together, using a wide range of materials—play dough, finger paint, clay, and cotton balls. Talk about the different textures, encouraging your child to examine how the materials feel, how they look, and how they can be used. Art can be a social and therapeutic experience. It can help your child develop fine motor skills, eye-hand coordination, and problem-solving skills. The activities in this chapter will give your child and other family members a chance to create a product that is uniquely their own.

Select activities that match the ability level and interests of your child. Offer assistance only when he needs it. All of these activities can be done in a group or family setting or with an adult and child, each participant creating a unique masterpiece. Have fun creating, building, and expanding your imagination! Here to help you Pound 'n' Paint, Pour 'n' Create is the Violet Family.

The Violet Family Plays Pound 'n' Paint, Pour 'n' Create Games

Nicholas Violet is a rambunctious 7-year-old who loves to run and play. But Nicholas has learning disabilities that make it difficult for him to learn like other children his age. He also has emotional problems which affect most of his interactions with other people. He can speak well and is capable of doing many of the same activities as other children his age. However, his emotional problems inhibit his ability to participate with other children in group games. He often becomes frustrated, anxious, and angry.

Nicholas needs to have positive and successful play experiences to help him learn how to play with other children. Art activities give him the opportunity to express himself and successfully participate in a group situation. With art there are no right and wrong answers—no judgments.

Nicholas's sister, Patty, and brother, Brian, love to explore different art activities at home with Nicholas. They help him learn that he does not have to be afraid to try and that he can have fun creating his own unique designs.

How to Make Play Clay and Play Clay Fun

These are the ingredients you'll need for play clay activities:

   ☆ Rolling pin
   ☆ Garlic press

☆ Cookie cutters, bottle caps, stones from outdoors
☆ Toy tea set or kitchen utensils
☆ Homemade play clay or modeling clay

Here is the recipe you'll need to make inedible play clay:

☆ 1 cup flour
☆ 1/2 cup salt

☆ 1/4 cup water

☆ Food coloring

Mix flour and salt, then slowly add colored water. Knead well. Objects made from this mixture can be left out to harden. Store unused clay in an airtight container.

Here is the recipe you'll need to make edible play clay:

☆ 1 cup smooth peanut butter

☆ 2/3 cup crunchy cereal

☆ 1 cup powdered milk

Mix well, play with, then eat.

Play Clay Zoo Fun

Patty and Brian help Nicholas make his own play clay. His favorite is the peanut butter kind. He thinks it's great fun to eat his masterpieces for a snack. The children create a play clay zoo by molding the clay into different animal shapes. When you do this activity with your child, talk as you play, encouraging him to "pinch," "pound," "roll," and "pat" the clay into different shapes. Roll out clay on the table. Use cookie cutters and bottle cap tops to make different shapes. Assist your child if necessary. Squeeze play clay through a garlic press; feel the textures and make a comparison to spaghetti. Have a make-believe dinner. Mold clay into pretend hamburgers, peas, and french fries. Have a tea party using your newly created food and a toy tea set. Make a birthday cake, pretend to blow out the candles, and eat the cake.

Adaptation for the Physically Impaired.   If your child is physically unable to do any more than hold or touch the clay, you can play for him, using his imagination. Make him an active participant by letting him direct your actions. Ask questions such as, "Should we make a snake or an elephant? Do you want big ears or little ears, a tail or no tail?"

Baker's Clay Fun

These are the ingredients you'll need for this activity:

☆ 4 cups flour

☆ 1 to 2 cups salt

- ☆ 1-1/2 cups water
- ☆ Cookie cutters
- ☆ Paints, food coloring
- ☆ Brush, felt-tip pens

Mix dry ingredients, then add water gradually. Knead for 5 minutes. Cut or mold into shapes. Bake on cookie sheet at 350 degrees for 45 to 60 minutes. Clay is done when light brown and slightly hard. Clay will harden further when taken from the oven. Decorate clay shapes with paints, felt-tip pens, or food coloring. Store unbaked clay unrefrigerated in a plastic bag.

Sawdust Clay Fun

These are the ingredients you'll need for this activity:

- ☆ Sawdust
- ☆ Wallpaper paste
- ☆ Water
- ☆ Tempera paint
- ☆ Paintbrush

Mix equal parts sawdust, wallpaper paste, and water. Add more water if the consistency is too sticky. Mold into various shapes and allow clay to dry. Paint the hardened shape.

How to Make Finger Paint Fun

These are the ingredients you'll need for this activity:

- ☆ 1 cup liquid starch
- ☆ Containers
- ☆ 6 cups water
- ☆ Food coloring
- ☆ 1/2 cup soap flakes (*not* detergent)
- ☆ Finger paint paper

Dissolve the soap flakes in 2 cups of water until no lumps remain, then mix well with the starch and remaining water. Pour equal amounts into containers, one for each color, and add food coloring. You may add powdered paint to the mixture. Place paint on finger paint paper. Enjoy making patterns in the finger paint with hands, fingers, or even feet!

Adaptation for the Physically Impaired.   Some children will find it easier to "toe" paint than to finger paint. Many children can finger paint much better if the paper is taped to the table surface.

Adaptation for the Visually Impaired.   Add sand, salt, or coffee grinds to the finger paint recipe for a change of texture.

SAFETY NOTE

For younger children, substitute a food-based paint for a toxic or soap-based paint, since most young children explore with their mouths. See Pudding Paint Fun in this chapter or Shaving Cream Masterpiece games in chapter 1 (pages 28-29).

Squeeze Painting Fun

These are the ingredients you'll need for these activities:

- ☆ Empty plastic glue bottles
- ☆ Plastic bags
- ☆ Tape
- ☆ Tempera paints or mustard, ketchup, and mayonnaise
- ☆ Cotton swabs, popsicle sticks, or spoons
- ☆ Container of water
- ☆ Drawing paper or plain paper towels
- ☆ Fine-point markers
- ☆ Eyedropper or cooking baster
- ☆ Newspaper

Put small amounts of finger paint or ketchup, mustard, and mayonnaise in plastic bags—enough to completely fill the bag when flat. Tape the bags closed. Show your child how to squeeze and press the paint in different directions to make unique designs. Use cotton swabs, popsicle sticks, or spoons to create different patterns. Erase any painting by smoothing over the bag with your fingers.

Or dampen a piece of paper and lay it on newspaper. Squeeze some globs of paint from a plastic glue bottle onto the paper. Let the paint soak and spread for a few seconds, then add other colors. When the paint and paper are dry, add designs or details with fine-point markers.

You can provide sturdy containers of slightly thickened tempera and an assortment of different-sized droppers or basters. Drop paint onto construction paper to make designs.

Pudding Paint Fun

These are the ingredients you'll need for this activity:

- ☆ Box of pudding
- ☆ Acrylic cutting board or other smooth washable surface
- ☆ Popsicle sticks

Prepare pudding as directed. Put approximately ½ cup of pudding on a smooth surface. Help your child explore the pudding with his hands and fingers just as he would finger paint. Use a popsicle stick to make designs. This will be a fun activity because it not only feels good but tastes good too!

Adaptation for the Visually Imapaired. Use a background that contrasts strongly with the pudding.

How to Make Collages and Collage Fun

Making collages is another way you and your child can explore the world inside your house.

Popcorn or Cotton Collage Fun

These are the ingredients you'll need for this activity:

- ☆ Liquid white glue
- ☆ Colored construction paper
- ☆ Cotton balls or popped popcorn
- ☆ Stencils of animals, food, or geometric shapes

Outline a design on the construction paper using a template or your own creative hand. Dribble glue inside the form. Press the popcorn or cotton onto the wet glue. Let dry. Add designs with crayons or colored markers. Nicholas especially likes to make snow scenes with cotton.

Styrofoam Collage Fun

These are the ingredients you'll need for this activity:

- ☆ Styrofoam meat tray
- ☆ Liquid white glue
- ☆ Styrofoam packing pieces
- ☆ Cut-up ribbons, tissue paper, and yarn
- ☆ Noodles, rice, beans, and seeds

Dribble glue over a Styrofoam meat tray, then place various pieces of Styrofoam, ribbon, and yarn on the wet glue. Let dry to form a collage. You can repeat this procedure using noodles, rice, beans, and seeds.

Object Sculpture Fun

These are the ingredients you'll need for this activity:

☆ Styrofoam pieces, scrap wood, pipe cleaners, popsicle sticks, corks, spools, and other odds and ends

☆ Liquid white glue

☆ Boxes of various sizes

Build a sculpture by gluing together a variety of items. Smaller items like spools or straws can be glued to larger wood scraps. Empty cereal, jewelry, or toothpick boxes can be glued together for a paper box sculpture.

Kitchen Collage Fun

These are the ingredients you'll need for this activity:

☆ Cardboard box top or Styrofoam meat tray

☆ Paste or glue

☆ Spaghetti, macaroni, dried beans, rice, artificially colored cereal, clean eggshells, and popcorn

Create a design on a cardboard box top. Arrange various food ingredients into an interesting design and glue the pieces in place. Hang this creative design on a kitchen wall or window.

Simple 'n' Fun Craft Projects

These activities will develop your child's creativity and provide many ways for your family to create together.

Mittens Fun

Trace around your child's hands to make two mitten shapes. Cut the mittens out and decorate them with crayons. Paste onto a larger piece of construction paper and glue a piece of yarn from one mitten to the other. Label right- and left-hand mittens. To help your child learn which is which, ask him to put each hand on the appropriate mitten.

Spring Flowers Fun

Cut out stems and leaves from construction paper. Use 2 to 4 cupcake papers for the blossom, placing one inside the other. Paste onto pastel-colored construction paper, and use crayons to draw in grass and sunshine.

Snowman Fun

Paste three white paper lace doilies onto construction paper. Use crayons or cut out shapes from construction paper to add features, such as a hat, stick, arms, buttons, boots, and scarf.

Cotton Candy Fun

Place pink chalk into a zip-lock plastic bag. Crush the chalk into a fine powder. Put cotton into the bag and shake until the cotton has turned pink. Roll a piece of paper into a cone shape and tape the base closed. Place the cotton in the cone. You can also use tan or brown construction paper to make ice cream cones and different-colored chalk to color cotton ice cream.

SAFETY NOTE

Be sure your child does not inhale the chalk dust.

Body Shape Fun

These are the ingredients you'll need for this activity:

 ☆ Large pieces of brown paper, butcher paper, or newspaper
 ☆ Crayons
 ☆ Stapler

Have your child lie on a large piece of paper. A parent, brother, or sister traces the outline of his body. After his body is traced on paper, discuss and paint or color the different body parts and clothing. Encourage him to take notice of important body parts such as his mouth, nose, and ears, as well as clothing. Repeat, staple the two outlines together, and stuff with crumpled newspaper to make a three-dimensional body drawing.

Picture Paperweight Fun

These are the ingredients you'll need for this activity:

☆ Bowl
☆ 1/4 cup powdered tempera paint
☆ 1/4 cup liquid white glue
☆ Piece of waxed paper
☆ 3/4-inch-wide primary paintbrush
☆ Smooth flat rock
☆ Photo of your child or a favorite person

Mix the tempera paint and glue together in a bowl. Paint rock with tempera-glue mixture. Press photo on the wet rock and allow ample time to dry. Nicholas, Brian, and Patty made these paperweights to give to their grandparents.

Paperweight Sandcasting Fun

These are the ingredients you'll need for this activity:

- ☆ Beach or commercial sand
- ☆ Shoe box
- ☆ Coffee can
- ☆ Mixing spoon
- ☆ Aluminum foil
- ☆ Water
- ☆ Powdered plaster of paris
- ☆ Tempera paint

Press a sheet of aluminum foil into a shoe box, molding it to fit. Line the inside completely. Fill the box a little more than half full with damp sand. The sand should be just wet enough to hold together. Place your child's bare hand or foot in the sand and press down hard to form a well-defined hand or footprint. Put plaster of paris in an old coffee can and slowly add water to the powder while stirring. The plaster should have the consistency of thin cream.

Pour the liquid plaster of paris into the foot or handprint. You must work quickly as plaster hardens very fast. Do not let it overflow. Let plaster dry for one week.

After a week, take out the hardened foot or handprint. Brush away any loose sand. Have your child place his foot or hand on the print to help refresh his memory from the week before. To enhance the foot or handprint, your child can paint it his favorite color. Use the coated print as a paperweight or gift for a favorite relative.

Family Tree Fun

These are the ingredients you'll need for this activity:

- ☆ Light-colored construction paper
- ☆ Finger paint
- ☆ Crayon or felt-tip pen

Draw a tree with many branches on the paper. Have each family member place a thumb in the finger paint and make a thumbprint on a branch. Using a crayon or felt-tip pen, add eyes, nose, mouth, and any other body parts to the thumbprint. Write each person's name under his/her thumbprint and you'll have a family tree.

Object Printing Fun

These are the ingredients you'll need for this activity:

- ☆ Absorbent construction paper
- ☆ Colored tempera paints
- ☆ Sponges
- ☆ Paintbrush
- ☆ Printing objects—vegetables or fruits (e.g., potatoes, apples, carrots, celery cut into sections), hair curlers, sponges, nails, bolts, plastic table toys, paper cup rim, teeth of a comb

Apply liquid tempera to a damp sponge with the paintbrush. Press an object onto the painted sponge. Use the object to stamp the shape onto the paper. Repeat with different objects and colors. The Violets make this activity a family project with everyone working cooperatively to create a mural on a large sheet of paper.

Funny Faces Activity

These are the ingredients you need for this activity:

- ☆ Old magazines
- ☆ Heavy white paper

☆ Paste

☆ Yarn

☆ Crayons

Cut out an assortment of eyes, ears, noses, and mouths from large pictures of people in magazines. Include lots of different types of facial features to select from. Draw a circle on a heavy piece of white paper and paste in facial features. Hair, mustache, eyebrows, earrings, and other accessories can be colored in or added with yarn.

Stick Family Activity

These are the ingredients you'll need for this activity:

☆ Heavy cardboard

☆ Wiggly eyes (available in toy or fabric stores)

☆ Popsicle sticks

☆ Twigs gathered from outside

☆ Liquid white glue

☆ Black magic marker

Help your child glue twigs, each representing a member of the family, onto a piece of cardboard. Glue wiggly eyes at the top of the twigs and use a popsicle stick as a label for the top of the board. Write "Our Family" on the popsicle stick. Write the names of each family member under each figure and draw other body parts, such as arms and legs.

Tissue Blossoms Activity

These are the ingredients you need for this activity:

☆ Liquid white glue

☆ Large piece of construction paper

☆ Pieces of colored tissue paper cut into 1/2- to 1-inch squares

Draw a springtime design (e.g., flower, tree) on construction paper. Pour a small amount of glue over the design. Crumple tissue paper and press onto the design until the design is completely filled in by tissue paper.

Butterfly Mobiles Activity

These are the ingredients you'll need for this activity:

☆ Bright-colored construction paper
☆ Bright-colored fabric or wallpaper remnants
☆ Paste
☆ Crayons
☆ Colored yarn

Trace around each family member's feet on a piece of construction paper. These will be the butterflies' wings. Draw the butterflies' bodies between the two wings. Cut out the butterflies and paste two narrow strips of construction paper in place for the antennae. Decorate the butterflies with bits of bright fabric or construction paper. Tie them to a hanger with colored yarn.

Screen Painting Fun

These are the ingredients you'll need for this activity:

☆ A piece of screen
☆ Tempera paints or food coloring
☆ An old toothbrush
☆ Drawing paper
☆ Newspaper
☆ Cut-out shapes, leaves, or other objects

Cover work area with newspaper. Hold the screen over a piece of paper. Dip the toothbrush in paint and brush it on the screen so the paint splatters through the screen onto the paper. Wash the brush and splatter with a new color. Or lay a cut-out shape, leaf, or object on top of the paper. Splatter paint over the paper, with or without the screen. Remove the object, select a new one, and repeat with a different color of paint.

Paint Magic Fun

These are the ingredients you'll need for this activity:

☆ White construction paper
☆ White crayon or candle
☆ Liquid tempera paint

Draw invisible designs with white crayon or candles on paper. Paint the surface with tempera paint. Watch the pictures appear!

Crayon Resist Fun

These are the ingredients you'll need for this activity:

- ☆ Crayons
- ☆ Dark-colored tempera paint, diluted
- ☆ White construction paper

Create a design on white construction paper with colored crayons. Press hard, making deep, rich colors. When everyone in your family finishes his drawing, he should paint all over and around it with a thin solution of dark paint. The dark paint fills in all the areas that the crayons missed. In the areas covered with crayon, the crayon resists the paint. Watch and discuss the changes that occur.

Abstract Painting Activity

These are the ingredients you'll need for this activity:

- ☆ Black posterboard cut into 8-inch by 12-inch pieces
- ☆ Blue, yellow, red, and green enamel paint
- ☆ Squeeze bottles
- ☆ Gold and silver glitter

Put the different-colored paints into individual squeeze bottles. Demonstrate for your child how to squeeze the paint from the bottle onto the posterboard, one time across for each color. Remind or help your child to keep his hand in motion constantly so that each color will be spread throughout the picture. After all the colors have been used, sprinkle gold and silver glitter on the wet design. Allow time for the painting to dry, and then mount it on a white background.

Christmas Holiday Decoration Fun

These are the ingredients you'll need for this activity:

- ☆ Cardboard tubes from toilet paper
- ☆ Tempera paint

☆ Paintbrush

☆ Heavy-duty string

☆ Clear liquid glue

☆ Colored glitter

Paint designs on the cardboard tubes and allow time to dry. Dab clear liquid glue on one tube at a time and sprinkle on glitter. String all the tubes together. Loop the string around the first and last tube and tie to secure all the rolls onto the string. Hang on your Christmas tree or on the wall as a holiday decoration.

Template Coloring Fun

These are the ingredients you'll need for this activity:

☆ Templates

☆ Crayons

☆ Large manila coloring paper or newsprint

Use commercially made templates or cut your own shapes from cardboard. Templates can include basic shapes (circle, square, triangle, rectangle), or, for more interesting drawings, use shapes like a star, heart, car, boat, airplane, dog, horse, or butterfly. Place the template under a piece of coloring paper or newsprint and color over the top with a crayon.

Rub-a-Print Fun

These are the ingredients you'll need for this activity:

☆ Light-colored construction paper

☆ Crayons

☆ Objects—leaves, coins, keys, combs, or other textured objects

Explore textures with this game. Place construction paper over objects and color on top of the paper with a crayon. The colored rubbing will produce a textured crayon design of the object under the paper. Discuss how the texture looks.

Family Sand Mural Fun

These are the ingredients you'll need for this activity:

- ☆ Large piece of construction or butcher paper
- ☆ White glue
- ☆ Colored sand

The Violets like to create a rainbow mural. Everyone takes a turn at spreading glue onto paper. Working together, each family member drops a bit of colored sand onto the glue. Shake off the extra sand; the result is a beautiful design that everyone worked together to make. Make colored sand by mixing clean sand with liquid tempera paint. When it dries, sift it through a screen.

Adaptation for the Visually Impaired.   Use different shapes of pasta to make the mural.

Tie-Dye Fun

These are the ingredients you'll need for this activity:

- ☆ Four small bowls of water
- ☆ Food coloring—green, red, yellow, and blue
- ☆ Coffee filters

Place a different color in each bowl of water. The water will turn rich shades of green, red, yellow, and blue. Crumple a coffee filter and dip part of it into one color. Squeeze out the excess water and repeat the process, dipping a different part of the filter into each color. Flatten the filter and let it dry. Hang the tie-dyed filters in the window and enjoy the sunlight as it comes through the rainbow of colors.

India Ink Design Fun

These are the ingredients you'll need for this activity:

- ☆ India ink or diluted tempera paint
- ☆ Eyedropper
- ☆ Straw

☆ Light-colored construction paper

☆ Watercolors

Drop several drops of India ink onto the paper with an eyedropper. Blow through the straw to spread the ink. Blowing creates interesting line designs that look like tree trunks and branches. After the ink has dried, paint with watercolor or brightly colored tempera paint to make colorful trees.

Yarn Design Fun

These are the ingredients you'll need for this activity:

☆ Colored yarn cut into various lengths between 2 and 8 inches

☆ Clear or white glue

☆ Pencil or crayon

☆ Manila or colored construction paper

Draw a simple design or favorite picture on construction paper. Trace over the design with glue, a small part at a time so that the glue does not dry, and place the yarn over the glue as you go along. Allow time to dry.

Crayon Etching Fun

These are the ingredients you'll need for this activity:

☆ Smooth paper, such as finger paint paper

☆ Crayons

☆ Paper towel

☆ Old fork, hairpin, or nail

☆ Black tempera paint (optional)

Use a variety of colored crayons to color heavily the entire surface of a small piece of paper or a marked-off area. Then color over the bottom layer with a black crayon. Rub the top layer with a paper towel to buff. Use a fork, hairpin, nail, or other pointed object to scratch away the surface, exposing the underlying colors and creating a design. Black tempera paint can be used instead of black crayon.

Butterfly Blot Fun

These are the ingredients you'll need for this activity:

☆ Medium sized construction paper

☆ Tempera paint

☆ Paintbrushes

☆ Mustard or catsup squeeze dispenser bottles

Help your child fold a piece of paper in half. Use a paintbrush or squeeze bottle to drop wet paint on one half of the paper, one color at a time. Fold the paper in half and rub. This will blot the wet side onto the dry side, creating a mirror image. Repeat with other colors, one at a time. Too many colors will cause the design to lose its effectiveness. Drops of white paint added after all the other colors have been used will help set off the contrast of colors. The blots can also be made with all colors used at once.

String Painting Fun

These are the ingredients you'll need for this activity:

☆ Manila construction paper, medium sized

☆ Various lengths of string and yarn

☆ Tempera paint

☆ Bowls for paint

Fold and crease a piece of paper lengthwise. Dip a piece of string or yarn into the paint. Place the wet yarn or string on one side of the paper in any pattern and fold the other side over it. Hold one hand on the paper over the string, and pull the string out through the fold with the other hand. Use one piece of string at a time. A variation of this activity is to experiment with string and paint on an open piece of paper, creating abstract designs.

Cut and Paste Fun

These are the ingredients you'll need for this activity:

☆ Children's or adaptive scissors

☆ Colored construction paper

☆ Tagboard or posterboard cut into the shape of a house

Help your child cut out various traced shapes, such as triangles, squares, circles, and rectangles from different colors of construction paper. Paste these shapes onto a house cut out from posterboard. For a more abstract, creative Cut and Paste activity, cut out a very large shape from posterboard. Allow your child the freedom to cut a variety of shapes and to experiment with placing the shapes in different ways to create his own unique designs.

Creating With Shapes Fun

These are the ingredients you'll need for this activity:

- ☆ Colored construction paper
- ☆ Scissors
- ☆ Paste
- ☆ Crayons or felt-tip pens

Cut various shapes out of construction paper—circles, half-circles, triangles, squares, and rectangles. Use the shapes to trace simple pictures, such as a sailboat, a duck, or a house, onto a piece of paper. Your child can match and paste the correct shapes onto the paper, and he will have a ready-made picture to hang in his room.

Simple 'n' Fun Decorations and Toy Creations

These activities will allow your child to create decorations, toys, and ornaments for personal and family enjoyment.

Jewels 'n' Things Fun

These are the ingredients you'll need for this activity:

- ☆ 30-inch or longer shoelace
- ☆ Variety of large macaroni with large holes
- ☆ Fat, colored drinking straws cut into 1-inch lengths
- ☆ Dry cereal with large holes

Tie pieces of macaroni to one end of the shoelace to keep the other pieces from falling off. String various items onto the shoelace. Tie the ends of the shoelace together to make a beautiful necklace or bracelet.

Marshmallow Dog

These are the ingredients you'll need for this activity:

- ☆ Regular and miniature marshmallows or scraps of Styrofoam
- ☆ Toothpicks
- ☆ Colored construction paper
- ☆ Gel icing in a tube
- ☆ Tape

Create a dog by putting two regular-size marshmallows together with toothpicks. Form the head with another marshmallow and toothpicks. Attach the head slightly higher than the rest of the body. Make each leg from two miniature marshmallows on a toothpick. Attach four legs to the body, two to the bottom of each marshmallow. Make the nose, tail, and two ears with miniature marshmallows. Attach to the body with toothpicks. Draw gel icing eyes. Try your hand at a snowman, a little boy or girl, or a favorite animal. Styrofoam pieces can be substituted for marhsmallows.

Snowman Ornament Activity

These are the ingredients you'll need for this activity:

- ☆ Eggbeater
- ☆ Equal amounts of soap flakes and water
- ☆ Black tempera paint
- ☆ Paintbrush
- ☆ Yarn or fabric strips
- ☆ Construction paper
- ☆ Outlined form of snowman on cardboard

Mix water and soap flakes with an eggbeater until the mixture is very stiff. Everyone can take turns mixing, although for safety reasons, young children should be assisted by an adult. Give your child a chance to feel the texture of this mixture. Spoon the mixture onto the outline of the snowman. Spread evenly and let dry overnight. The next day, decorate the snowman by painting on eyes, nose, and mouth with black tempera paint. Glue on a construction paper top hat and fabric strips for a scarf. These materials can be used to make a variety of designs besides a snowman.

Spring Chicks Activity

These are the ingredients you'll need for this activity:

- ☆ Styrofoam egg carton
- ☆ Black and orange construction paper

☆ Liquid white glue

☆ Cotton balls

Cut individual cups from the egg carton for each family member. Help your child cut two small eyes from the black construction paper and one orange triangle for the beak. Dip a cotton ball into glue and stick it into the cup. Place glue on the beak and eyes and stick them on the cotton ball. Repeat to create a family of spring chicks.

How to Make Puppets and Puppet Fun

These activities develop creativity as you help your child create the puppets and later as you both play with them. See individual recipes for ingredients.

Paper Bag Puppet

(Ingredients: Paper bags, paints or crayons, colored paper, yarn, buttons, newspaper, other odds and ends for the face, glue and/or a stapler) Stuff a paper bag with newspaper. Glue or staple closed. Glue on bits of yarn for hair, buttons or construction paper for eyes and other facial features, or decorate the puppet's face with crayons. Staple a second paper bag to the first, leaving room for the child's hand to slip in and work the puppet.

Hand Puppet

(Ingredients: Child's hand, nontoxic felt-tip pens) Create a puppet by using felt-tip pens to draw a face on one finger or on the palm of the hand. Children love this and can play make-believe with this puppet or any of the others. For easy cleanup, use watercolor markers.

Paper Plate Puppet

(Ingredients: Two white paper plates, glue, stapler or tape, crayons, felt-tip pens or paint, scissors, construction paper, yarn, old earrings, scraps of fabric, other odds and ends) Decorate the back of one plate with a face. Use crayons or paint to make eyes, nose, and mouth. Cut the other paper plate in half. Glue, tape, or staple it to

the face plate so that the fronts of the plates are facing each other. This will give you a space for your hand. Use some of the other ingredients to decorate the puppet. You can cut a small hole for the mouth and stick your finger through it for a tongue.

Puppet Play Fun

These are the ingredients you'll need for this activity:

- ☆ Puppet(s)
- ☆ Puppet stage—a cut-out opening in an old sheet, towel, or large sturdy box
- ☆ A small group of children

Your child can act out his favorite story with a puppet. He can be an elephant, a kitten, a puppy, a mom or dad, or just a little boy. Often his puppet becomes an extension of himself; he will express his own thoughts and ideas through the puppet's conversation. With encouragement from their parents, Nicholas, Brian, and Patty often act out a story or skit. The children make the puppets run, dance, sing, or do things the children usually do during a typical day.

Show Your Family Art

Once you, your child, and other family members have experienced the world of arts and crafts by trying a few of the activities described in this chapter, have a family art show. Display your works of art. Cut inexpensive mats out of posterboard for drawings, collages, and other paper art. Tape pictures to the backs of the mats and then to the wall with masking tape. Place three-dimensional objects on sheets of colored construction paper. Invite everyone to "ooh" and "ah" over the masterpieces.

Chapter 6

EXPLORING THE WORLD OF MUSIC AND RHYTHM

Music is a joyous way for children to express themselves and create sounds and rhythms. Combine words and music into a song. Tell a story in melody and rhyme. Have fun with finger play and rhythm games. Dance and movement to music are universal forms of expression. Music is communication that appeals to people of all ages, from infants to grandparents. It spans all physical and social ability levels, making it an activity the whole family can enjoy.

Children with disabilities are no exception. Whatever their learning or physical problems, children can enjoy music. A child without hearing will be able to feel the vibrations of a drum and will use her sense of vision and touch to compensate for her hearing loss. A child with a visual impairment can be guided physically or with words through a music or rhythm activity. A child without the use of her lower limbs can swing her arms and clap her hands, use percussion instruments, or move or be pushed in her wheelchair in time to music. If your child cannot move her arms and hands, you can move them for her and swing her to the rhythm.

The activities in this chapter will help your child develop body awareness and a sense of self; develop important language skills and concepts; develop creativity and spontaneity; increase music appreciation; improve large and small muscle control; develop endurance; discriminate sounds, tempos, and melodies; follow directions; and gain a sense of rhythm and an understanding of sequence of actions.

These activities are structured to help stimulate your own ideas and imagination. Do not overlook the importance of approval and an atmosphere of freedom to help your child be creative. It is not as important for your child to master these games as it is for her to participate in and enjoy what she is doing.

If your child is physically or hearing impaired, some general adaptations to keep in mind throughout the activities in this chapter include:

- When singing songs or chants, tap the rhythm lightly on some part of your child's body, or bounce your child on your knee to the beat of the music.
- Use a drum or bells and help your child keep rhythm to the songs you sing.
- An adult can help the child, one-on-one, to make the appropriate response.
- Actions or responses can be adapted to be as simple as smiling, blinking, waving, or raising a hand.
- Promote your child's self-concept and body awareness by touching the parts of her body that are mentioned in the songs and finger-play games you sing.

Participation levels may vary from one child to the next. Some children may be able to participate verbally, but not physically, while others may be better able to participate physically than verbally. The important ingredient in participation is fun and enjoyment, whether your child needs physical assistance, sign language, or guidance through an entire activity. We call these activities Rap 'n' Rhyme, Music Time. Here to show you how to play them is the Red family.

The Red Family Plays
Rap 'n' Rhyme, Music Time Games

Carmen Red is bright, talkative, animated, and outgoing. She often seems older than 8 years old. Carmen has spina bifida, a congenital defect that has left her paralyzed from the waist down. She uses a wheelchair to move around.

Carmen lives with her parents, two older brothers, Mario and Tony, and her grandparents. The family loves to go on outings together, and they lavish lots of attention on Carmen. In fact, if she weren't such an even-tempered child, "Carmen would be spoiled," Mrs. Red says with a smile. "She is," Mario insists.

Carmen stops the discussion with a favorite family request: "Let's sing some songs!"

Rhythm and Finger Play Songs and Games

Finger play games will enhance your child's language and motor development. Finger play also provides an opportunity to stimulate imagination and social interaction. If your child lacks the hand function and coordination for the finger play games, let her do the best she can. She'll enjoy the music and have fun watching your hand movements. You, your child, and other family members should play these games in a relaxed atmosphere.

These finger play games and songs may already be old favorites in your family. Use a rhythmic chant for these games, add a familiar melody, or use the suggested tunes. You'll be pleased with the results.

Pat-a-Cake Song

PAT-A-CAKE, PAT-A-CAKE, BAKER'S MAN, BAKE ME A CAKE AS FAST AS YOU CAN!

Clap hands together or move your child's hands in a clapping motion.

ROLL IT AND PAT IT, AND MARK IT WITH "B" (or use your child's initial).

Make a rolling motion, then a pat, and write initial in the air.

PUT IT IN THE OVEN FOR BABY AND ME.

Clap hands together.

Eentsy-Weentsy Spider Song

THE EENTSY-WEENTSY SPIDER WENT UP THE WATER SPOUT.

Touch thumb of one hand against forefinger of the other; swivel fingers alternately to climb up the spout.

DOWN CAME THE RAIN AND WASHED THE SPIDER OUT.

Show rain coming down with fingers held up high and then trickling down to lap; cross hands and show a sweeping motion out to show the rain washing the spider out.

OUT CAME THE SUN AND DRIED UP ALL THE RAIN.

Make a big circle with both hands clasped over head.

NOW THE EENTSY-WEENTSY SPIDER WENT UP THE SPOUT AGAIN.

Repeat action of first line.

With a baby, use your fingers in a walking motion and simply climb up and down the baby's arm or body.

I'm a Little Teapot Song

I'M A LITTLE TEAPOT SHORT AND STOUT.

Act short and stout.

HERE IS MY HANDLE, HERE IS MY SPOUT.

Place one hand on hip, extend other arm, elbow and wrist bent out like a spout.

WHEN I GET ALL STEAMED UP THEN I SHOUT

TIP ME OVER AND POUR ME OUT!

Tip sideways in direction of extended arm.

I'M A VERY SPECIAL POT IT IS TRUE.

HERE LET ME SHOW WHAT I CAN DO.

I CAN CHANGE MY HANDLE AND MY SPOUT.

Reverse hand on hip and extended arm to other side.

TIP ME OVER AND POUR ME OUT!

Tip in the new direction of the spout.

Apples Song
(Melody: "Hush Little Baby")

WAY UP HIGH IN THE APPLE TREE

Raise hands above head.

TWO LITTLE APPLES SMILED AT ME.

Hands still raised, make a fist to represent apple.

I SHOOK THE TREE AS HARD AS I COULD.

Shake body and arms.

DOWN FELL THE APPLES.

Lower hands.

MMMM! THEY'RE GOOD!

Take bite of "apple."

Five Little Monkeys Song
(A chant)

FIVE LITTLE MONKEYS HOPPING ON THE BED.

Make five fingers of one hand jump on palm of other hand.

ONE FELL OFF AND BUMPED HIS HEAD.

Hold up one finger and turn it to the side.

MAMA CALLED THE DOCTOR AND THE DOCTOR SAID,

Hold imaginary receiver to ear.

NO MORE MONKEYS JUMPING ON THE BED!

Shake finger and head.

Chant four more verses, with one less monkey each time. To make an action chant: Make a square with masking tape on the floor for a pretend bed. Have five friends or family members jump on "bed" and "fall" off one at a time as in the chant.

This Is the Circle That Is My Head Song
(Melody: "Hush Little Baby")

THIS IS THE CIRCLE THAT IS MY HEAD.

Raise arms above head to make circle.

THIS IS MY MOUTH WITH WHICH WORDS ARE SAID.

Point to mouth.

THESE ARE MY EYES WHICH I USE TO SEE.

Point to eyes.

THIS IS MY NOSE THAT IS PART OF ME.

Point to nose.

THIS IS THE HAIR THAT GROWS ON MY HEAD.

Point to hair.

THIS IS MY HAT ALL PRETTY AND RED.

Gesture with hands on head to suggest pointed hat.

THIS IS THE FEATHER SO BRIGHT AND GAY.

Use finger as feather.

NOW I'M READY FOR SCHOOL/BED/PLAY TODAY.

Get up and walk a few steps.

Place a large mirror in front of your child so she can see the body parts used in this song.

Ten Fingers Song
(A chant)

This game will increase your child's awareness of her fingers and different ways she can move them.

I HAVE TEN LITTLE FINGERS.

Hold up hands, open.

AND THEY ALL BELONG TO ME.

Point to self.

I CAN MAKE THEM DO THINGS. WOULD YOU LIKE TO SEE?

Point to eyes.

I CAN OPEN THEM UP WIDE.

Spread fingers.

SHUT THEM UP TIGHT.

Make tight fist.

PUT THEM TOGETHER.

Fold fingers together, and hide them behind your back.

I CAN JUMP THEM UP HIGH.

Reach above head.

I CAN JUMP THEM DOWN LOW.

Touch floor.

FOLD THEM QUIETLY.

Fold fingers/hands together.

AND SIT (OR STAND) THEM JUST SO.

Johnny Works With One Hammer Song
(A chant)

JOHNNY WORKS WITH ONE HAMMER,

Pound with one fist on knee.

ONE HAMMER, ONE HAMMER.

JOHNNY WORKS WITH ONE HAMMER,

THEN HE WORKS WITH TWO.

JOHNNY WORKS WITH TWO HAMMERS,

Pound with both fists on corresponding knees.

TWO HAMMERS, TWO HAMMERS.

JOHNNY WORKS WITH TWO HAMMERS,

THEN HE WORKS WITH THREE.

Repeat verse with three hammers. Stomp one foot along with hands. Repeat verse with four hammers. Stomp both feet with fists. Repeat verse with five hammers. Move head forward and backward in time to the rhythm.

Open, Shut Them Song
(A chant)

Use the words of this rhyme to tell you how to move your hands.

OPEN THEM, SHUT THEM,

OPEN THEM, SHUT THEM.

GIVE A LITTLE CLAP.

OPEN THEM, SHUT THEM,
OPEN THEM, SHUT THEM.
PUT THEM IN YOUR LAP.
CREEP THEM, CREEP THEM.
CREEP THEM, CREEP THEM.
RIGHT UP TO YOUR CHIN.
OPEN WIDE YOUR LITTLE MOUTH
BUT (PAUSE) DO NOT LET THEM IN.

Three Little Ducks Song
(A chant)

THREE LITTLE DUCKS THAT I ONCE KNEW.

Hold up three fingers.

A TALL ONE,

Stand up tall, or hold hands up high.

A SHORT ONE,

Squat down low or hold hands down low.

A FAT ONE, TOO!

Hands and arms open wide.

BUT THE ONE LITTLE DUCK WITH A FEATHER ON HER BACK,

Stand up, hold both hands behind your lower back to make a feather.

SHE RULED THE OTHERS WITH A QUACK, QUACK, QUACK.

Point fingers out, hold hands together flat, and open and close to make a quack.

A QUACK, QUACK, QUACK.

DOWN TO THE RIVER THEY WOULD GO,

WIBBLE, WABBLE, WIBBLE, WABBLE, TO AND FRO

Hands together in front of body weaving in and out of imaginary river.

BUT THE ONE LITTLE DUCK WITH THE FEATHER ON HER BACK,

Repeat previous action.

SHE RULED THE OTHERS WITH A QUACK, QUACK, QUACK,

A QUACK, QUACK, QUACK.

SHE RULED THE OTHERS WITH A QUACK, QUACK, QUACK.

Counting the Bunnies Song
(Melody: "Hush Little Baby")

MY BUNNIES MUST GO TO BED,

THE LITTLE MOTHER RABBIT SAID.

BUT I WILL COUNT THEM FIRST TO SEE

IF THEY HAVE ALL COME BACK TO ME.

ONE BUNNY, TWO BUNNIES, THREE BUNNIES DEAR,

FOUR BUNNIES, FIVE BUNNIES—YES, ALL HERE!

THEY ARE THE PRETTIEST THINGS ALIVE

MY BUNNIES ONE, TWO, THREE, FOUR, FIVE.

Touch fingers in turn as you count.

The Little Turtle Song
(A chant)

THERE WAS A LITTLE TURTLE.
HE LIVED IN A BOX.
  Hands open to show box.
HE SWAM IN A PUDDLE.
  Fingers of one hand wiggle in circle made of the other.
HE CLIMBED ON THE ROCKS.
HE SNAPPED AT A MOSQUITO.
  Fingers spread—then four fingers close over thumb.
HE SNAPPED AT THE FLEA.
  Repeat previous action.
HE SNAPPED AT THE MINNOW.
  Repeat previous action.
AND HE SNAPPED AT ME.
  Point to self.
HE CAUGHT THE MOSQUITO.
  Make catching motion.
HE CAUGHT THE FLEA.
  Same action as before.
HE CAUGHT THE MINNOW.
  Same action as before.
BUT HE DIDN'T CATCH ME.
  Shaking head, point to self.

Cookie Jar Song
(A chant)

I LOOKED IN THE COOKIE JAR AND WHAT DID I SEE,
A BIG ROUND COOKIE MOTHER PUT THERE FOR ME
  Form a circle with both hands.
MOTHER LOOKED IN THE COOKIE JAR,
BUT SHE DIDN'T SEE
THE BIG ROUND COOKIE SHE PUT THERE FOR ME
  Form circle again.

Action Songs and Chants

These games are excellent for developing coordination, a sense of rhythm, and body awareness. Many of the following activities call for the child to assume a specific position or stance; but remember, do all activities in a position that is safe and comfortable for your child.

Body Sounds Song
(A chant)

Do the actions the song calls for.
I TAP MY HEELS AND GO CLICK, CLICK, CLICK.
I SLAP MY KNEES AND GO SMACK, SMACK, SMACK.
I SLIDE MY FEET AND GO SCUFF, SCUFF, SCUFF,
SCUFF, SCUFF, SCUFF MY FEET.
I TAKE MY TONGUE AND GO CLICK, CLICK, CLICK.
I TAKE MY FEET AND GO STOMP, STOMP, STOMP.
STOMP, STOMP, STOMP MY FEET.
Think of and add your own body sounds to this chant.

If You're Happy Song
(A chant)

IF YOU'RE HAPPY AND YOU KNOW IT, CLAP YOUR HANDS!
Clap, clap!
IF YOUR'RE HAPPY AND YOU KNOW IT, CLAP YOUR HANDS!
Clap, Clap!
IF YOU'RE HAPPY AND YOU KNOW IT,
AND YOU REALLY WANT TO SHOW IT,
IF YOU'RE HAPPY AND YOU KNOW IT, CLAP YOUR HANDS!
Clap, clap!
Replace the action of clapping with other actions—stomping feet, patting knees, jumping up and down, touching your head. Use this song to identify actions associated with certain feelings.

Example

IF YOU'RE SAD AND YOU KNOW IT,
SAY BOO HOO.
   Echo boo hoo and wipe your eyes.
IF YOU'RE FRIGHTENED AND YOU KNOW IT,
SHAKE ALL OVER.
   Shake your body.
IF YOU'RE HUNGRY AND YOU KNOW IT,
EAT SOME FOOD.
   Pretend to eat.
IF YOU'RE TIRED AND YOU KNOW IT,
GO TO SLEEP.
   Pretend to sleep.

Where Is Song
(Melody: "Are You Sleeping?" or "Frere Jacques").

This song helps the child recognize and learn her name.

Adult sings: WHERE IS (NAME), WHERE IS (NAME)?

Child responds: HERE I AM, HERE I AM.

Adult sings: HOW ARE YOU TODAY? HOW ARE YOU TODAY?

Child responds: I AM FINE, I AM FINE.

Adult responds with child until song is learned.

Everyone in Carmen Red's family (even her grandparents) sit in a circle to sing and play. Mrs. Red acts as a leader and begins by singing, "Where is Carmen?" In response, Carmen points to herself and raises her hand. Sometimes she beats out her response on a musical instrument. Other family members point to or wave to her.

For the nonverbal child, you may sing, "There is (name)!" and point to her.

Give a Cheer Song
(Melody: "Twinkle, Twinkle, Little Star")

LOOK AT (NAME) SITTING IN HER CHAIR.
DOESN'T SHE LOOK PRETTY THERE?
HEY, EVERYBODY, GIVE A CHEER,
FOR (NAME) WHO'S SITTING IN HER CHAIR!

Color Song
(A chant)

(NAME) WORE HER GREEN PANTS, HER GREEN PANTS, HER GREEN PANTS.

(NAME) WORE HER GREEN PANTS AT HOME TODAY.

While sitting in a group, ask each family member: WHAT COLOR IS YOUR (CLOTHING ITEM)?

After the answer, recite the chant. Repeat until everyone has had a turn.

Goodbye or Goodnight Song
(Melody: "Goodnight Ladies")

GOODBYE (NAME), GOODBYE (NAME),

GOODBYE (NAME), GOODBYE (NAME),

IT'S TIME TO GO ON HOME.

This song can be used to help an individual child or group with transition or change. *Goodbye* can be replaced with *goodnight*, and *home* with *bed*.

Hands On Song
(A chant)

Do the actions the song calls for.

HANDS ON SHOULDERS, HANDS ON KNEES,

HANDS BEHIND YOU, IF YOU PLEASE.

TOUCH YOUR SHOULDERS, NOW YOUR NOSE,

NOW YOUR HAIR AND NOW YOUR TOES.

HANDS UP HIGH, AS BEFORE.

NOW CLAP WITH HANDS—ONE, TWO, THREE, FOUR.

Sing With Me Song

Chant or create your own melody.

SING WITH ME, DO-OH, DO-OH.

SING WITH ME, DO-OH, DO-OH,

SING WITH ME, DO-OH, DO-OH,

DO-OH, DO-OH, DO.

CLAP WITH ME, DO-OH, DO-OH.

CLAP WITH ME, DO-OH, DO-OH.
CLAP WITH ME, DO-OH, DO-OH.
DO-OH, DO-OH, DO.

Between each verse of this song, let a participant choose an action.

Creative Movement Music, Songs, and Games

These activities will help your child respond to and appreciate music and explore body direction in space to a rhythmic beat.

Free Flow Music Fun

These are the ingredients you'll need for this set of activities:

- ☆ Piano or recorded music
- ☆ Drum or other rhythm instrument
- ☆ Music: "Movin" by Hap Palmer (optional) For ordering information see the resource list at the end of the book.
- ☆ Suggested ingredients are hula hoops, scarves, strips of crepe paper

Your child, family, and friends begin by standing in a circle with plenty of space between each person. Play music and instruct everyone to listen carefully. Tell the group to get ready to move according to the directions you give.

As you lead the way, keep in mind your child's ability level. Think about the different parts of the body and the various ways to move them to follow the tempo and mood of the music. Some examples are to move arms above the head or below the knees, shake them out, bend knees, bend arms, and bend at the waist. You can also vary movements: walk, run, hop, jump, skip, gallop, slide . . . all without touching anyone else. Or you can change position in space: high, middle, low. Or change directions in space: forward, sideways, backward. You may want to change tempo: slow, quick. Or change mood: Make stiff, jerky, or swaying movements.

Pretend to Be Game

You and your child can pretend to be famous dancers, famous ath-
letes, trees in the wind, summer storms, robots, feathers, animals
(turtles, elephants, rabbits, ponies), balloons inflating, worms, tops
spinning, rubber bands, flowers blossoming, merry-go-round
horses, a marching band.

While moving to the music, make patterns in the air with colored
scarves or long strips of crepe paper. Beat a drum or other rhythm
instrument in accompaniment. Using the ideas suggested to
encourage a variety of movements and stimulate imagination, you
might say, "How about a sideways jump? A turning jump? A low
run? A fast walk?"

Divide everyone into groups of two or three people. Give each
group a hula hoop to use while moving to the music. Put the hula
hoop flat on the floor so that the group can walk around it, jump
in it, jump out of it, hold it in their hands as they skip around in
a circle, raise it high, lower it, and do other movements that require
cooperative effort.

For a child who hesitates to participate in this activity, demonstrate the movement and provide encouragement and even physical guidance. These activities may be difficult for many children

because most organized activities and games do not require a child to improvise, be spontaneous, or initiate her own movements. Help your child by repeating the same movements until she is comfortable with them. Once your child understands and becomes involved, she will invent her own movements. Then it is time for you to imitate her!

Statue Game

You will need a piano or recorded instrumental music. Family and friends stand in a circle in an open, spacious room. Explain to the group that when the music is playing, they are to move around the room in a circle. Their movement should be free-flowing, in rhythm to the music. When the music stops, they must freeze their movement and pretend to be statues. Quickly go around the room and let each person tell what his or her statue is. When the music starts again, everyone continues moving rhythmically until it stops again.

Space Game

These are the ingredients you'll need for this activity:

☆ Hula hoop or carpet square

☆ Drum

Everyone in the group selects a hula hoop or carpet square and stands in or on it. This will be her very own space. When the drumbeat starts, each person leaves her space and walks, skips, hops, or leaps around the outside of her space. When the drumbeat stops, each person must go back to her original space. The drumbeat can include both fast and slow tempos. The adult leader beating the drum can call out different ways for the group to move when they are outside of their spaces.

Musical Circle Games

These are the ingredients you'll need for these activities:

☆ Instrumental recorded music

☆ Parachute or large sheet cut into the shape of a circle

☆ Balloons or lightweight balls, such as sponge balls

Round and Round

The group spaces itself evenly around the parachute. An adult leads the chant as the group follows the directions:
THE CIRCLE GOES ROUND, GOES ROUND, GOES ROUND.
Repeat.
THE CIRCLE GOES IN, GOES IN, GOES IN.
Repeat.
THE CIRCLE GOES DOWN, GOES DOWN, GOES DOWN.
Repeat.
THE CIRCLE GOES UP, GOES UP, GOES UP.
Repeat.
THE CIRCLE GOES FAST, GOES FAST, GOES FAST.
Repeat.
THE CIRCLE GOES SLOW, GOES SLOW, GOES SLOW.
Repeat.
THE CIRCLE GOES LEFT, GOES LEFT, GOES LEFT.
Repeat.
THE CIRCLE GOES RIGHT, GOES RIGHT, GOES RIGHT.
Repeat.

Bounce Around, Up and Down Game

You will need at least four people for this activity. Place several balloons or lightweight balls on the parachute. The group waves the parachute up and down to the rhythm of music or a chant, attempting to keep all the balls on the parachute. Everyone must work together to stop the balls from bouncing off. The game ends when all the balls have fallen off.

Round the Village Song
(A chant)

Form a circle and join hands. Select one of the children to be "it." "It" stands outside the circle.

GO 'ROUND AND 'ROUND THE VILLAGE.
GO 'ROUND AND 'ROUND THE VILLAGE.
GO 'ROUND AND 'ROUND THE VILLAGE.
AS WE HAVE DONE BEFORE.

The person who is "it" walks, skips, or runs around the circle.

Children in the circle raise arms to form arches while the person who is "it" weaves in and out.

GO IN AND OUT THE WINDOW.
GO IN AND OUT THE WINDOW.
GO IN AND OUT THE WINDOW.
AS WE HAVE DONE BEFORE.
NOW COME AND FACE YOUR PARTNER.
NOW COME AND FACE YOUR PARTNER.
NOW COME AND FACE YOUR PARTNER.
AS WE HAVE DONE BEFORE.

The person who is "it" chooses a partner and stands facing the partner.

NOW FOLLOW ME DOWN TO LONDON.
NOW FOLLOW ME DOWN TO LONDON.
NOW FOLLOW ME DOWN TO LONDON.
AS WE HAVE DONE BEFORE.

The circle moves right or left with the person who is "it" and partner in the center. To play again, the person who was "it" returns to the circle and the partner becomes "it."

You can sing the song over and change partners until everyone has had a chance to be "it." The person who is "it" can be paired with an adult if he or she needs special assistance.

Rhythm and Musical Instrument Games

These activities will introduce your child to various musical instruments and promote perceptual-motor coordination, a sense of rhythm, and musical activity.

Baby Rhythm Game

These are the ingredients you'll need for this activity:

- ☆ Hand bells
- ☆ Hand shaker or rattles
- ☆ Finger cymbals
- ☆ Instrumental record with a distinct beat

Babies and very young children love to dance to the beat of music in your arms. Rock and sway to the rhythm with your baby. Recite a rhythmic chant to the beat of your dancing. Your baby will delight in the fun. When your baby is lying on her back or sitting, hand her bells or a shaker and let her shake or bang to the music. Show her how to play the finger cymbals, which will fit perfectly in her hands. She will love playing these simple games with you.

Rhythm Stick Game

Play this game to help your child understand basic directional concepts while integrating simple movements. These are the ingredients you'll need for this activity:

- ☆ Family and friends
- ☆ Drumsticks or paper towel tubes

One person leads the game. Give each family member a rhythm stick. Begin the following chant, encouraging everyone to join you in the action.

STICKS UP IN THE AIR—UP, UP, UP IN THE AIR.
STICKS DOWN ON THE FLOOR—DOWN, DOWN, DOWN ON THE FLOOR.
STICKS BEHIND YOUR BACK—BEHIND, BEHIND, BEHIND YOUR BACK.
STICKS IN FRONT OF YOU—FRONT, FRONT, FRONT OF YOU.
STICKS NEXT TO YOUR SIDE—NEXT, NEXT, NEXT TO YOUR SIDE.

STICKS ACROSS TO THE OTHER SIDE—ACROSS, ACROSS, ACROSS TO YOUR OTHER SIDE.

STICKS GO SIDE TO SIDE—TO SIDE, TO SIDE, TO SIDE.

Alternate sides.

STICKS OVER YOUR HEAD—OVER, OVER, OVER YOUR HEAD.

STICKS UNDER YOUR KNEES—UNDER, UNDER, UNDER YOUR KNEES.

The chant dictates where the stick goes. Include many repetitions to make sure the basic concepts are clear. Do one part of the chant at a time. Encourage other family members to take turns being the leader. If your child has difficulty understanding front and back, provide physical guidance, and use directions like "touch your tummy" and "touch your back." Try "tap your sticks together" or "tap your sister's knee."

Guide your special child's hands to match the chant until she understands the directional concepts and can do it by herself. After this activity becomes familiar and comfortable, give each person two sticks. The Reds find this can be great fun and encourages lots of family interaction.

Big Drum Beats, Little Drum Listens

This song provides lots of fun as it helps your child learn the concepts of big and little. These are the ingredients you'll need for this activity:

- ☆ Family and friends
- ☆ Two drums, pots, cans, or containers, one very big and one very small

Show both drums to your child and discuss the different sizes. Tell her you're going to beat the big drum. Now give her a turn and ask her to tell you what drum she is beating. Repeat with the little drum.

Sing the first part of the following chant and beat the big drum. Give each member of your family a turn while the little drum listens. Repeat this procedure with the second part of the chant. After everyone has had a turn, let individual players select the drum they would like to beat while joining the chant.

BIG DRUM BEATS, LITTLE DRUM LISTENS.
BIG DRUM BEATS, LITTLE DRUM HEARS.
LITTLE DRUM BEATS, BIG DRUM LISTENS.
LITTLE DRUM BEATS, BIG DRUM HEARS.

Carmen Red and her family sometimes play this game differently. They tape a different colored piece of construction paper onto the top of each drum. Then they replace the words "big" and "little" with the two colors. "Blue drum beats. Red drum listens."

Carmen's brother, Mario, and some of his friends play the game with her. They play the game by chanting, "Jim beats the drum. Carmen listens." Her brother Tony likes to hide the drums behind a screen and ask Carmen which drum he is beating. If your child needs extra help, ask her if she heard the big drum or the little one.

Adaptation for the Nonverbal Child. If your child is nonverbal and needs more help, bring both drums out from behind the screen and let her point to the one she heard. Or, make simple pictures of a big and little drum and ask her to point to the one she heard.

Carmen's grandmother likes to beat the drum twice quickly and wait for Carmen to repeat this. Or, twice slowly and wait for her to repeat that. Often Carmen chooses the rhythm.

The whole family likes to think of big things like mountains when Carmen beats the big drum and little things like pebbles when she beats the little drum.

Hit It One Time Game

This activity allows your child to follow directions with a simple motor response. You need only a drum, or other rhythm instrument.

(A Chant)
Verse 1: HIT IT ONE. HIT IT ONE. HIT IT ONE TIME.
Repeat 2 times.
HIT IT AGAIN AND AGAIN AND AGAIN AND AGAIN.
Verse 2; BRUSH IT ONE. BRUSH IT ONE. BRUSH IT ONE TIME.
Repeat 2 times.
BRUSH IT AGAIN AND AGAIN AND AGAIN AND AGAIN.

Demonstrate tapping the drum on the word "hit" and brushing the drum on the word "brush." Give each person a turn. Show your child how tapping and brushing feel different by demonstrating on her arm. Chant the first verse while passing the drum around a circle of family and friends. The person receiving the drum hits it one time and then passes it to the next person. Repeat until everyone has had a turn. Repeat the procedure, chanting the second verse in an almost-whisper. Tell players that when it is their turn, they need to brush it quietly. Change the order, "Hit" and "Brush."

Give each person the opportunity to add another way to hit the drum. Examples include these: "HIT IT *LOUD*," "HIT IT *quiet*," "HIT IT *FAST*," "HIT IT *S-L-O-W*." Follow the same procedure using other rhythm instruments, such as a tambourine, cymbal, tone block, or triangle.

Musical Instrument Chairs Game

This activity will introduce various types of instruments and promote perceptual-motor coordination, a sense of rhythm, and musical creativity. These are the ingredients you'll need for this activity:

☆ One chair per person

☆ One musical instrument for each chair

☆ A piano or instrumental recording

☆ Record player or tape recorder

Arrange the chairs in a circle. Place a musical instrument on each chair. Each member in the group selects a musical instrument, sits in the accompanying chair, and, when the music starts, begins playing the instrument. When the music stops, each player moves to the next chair and gets ready to play the new instrument as soon as the music starts again. A variation of this game is for everyone to play the musical instruments to the music while marching around the chairs. When the music stops, each person sits in the closest chair and exchanges instruments with the adjacent person. When the music starts, the group begins marching again.

Name the Instrument Game

This game will help your child develop listening skills and increase attention span and interest in what she hears. These are the ingredients you'll need for this activity:

☆ Several familiar instruments

☆ Pictures of instruments or duplicates of the instruments

Hide two to four instruments behind a screen or under a table. Place pictures or duplicates of the instruments on the table or in the middle of the circle where the group is sitting. Whoever is "it" plays one of the instruments out of sight, either behind the screen or under the table. "It" asks one of the other members of the group to guess which instrument was heard by selecting the matching instrument or picture. The child answering correctly becomes the new "it." To make the game more challenging, do not use duplicates or pictures of the instruments.

How to Make Instruments and Instrument Fun

You can make instruments out of common household ingredients. The whole family will enjoy creating their own instruments.

Making a Drum

You can make a drum from coffee cans, large vegetable cans, or oatmeal and salt boxes. Just remove the end of the can or box and cover the open end as tightly as possible with contact paper or inner tube rubber. If you use rubber, secure it with heavy cord or elastic. You can decorate your drums with paint or construction paper.

Making Rhythm Sticks

Use dowels of different thicknesses, and cut them to be approximately 12 inches long. Sand the ends, and paint or shellac the sticks.

Making Cymbals

Use two pot lids. Clash them together for a wonderful bang! Use all sizes of pot lids.

Making Rattles and Shakers

Use empty containers of various sizes (plastic spice bottles, film containers, bandage boxes, or two paper plates). Select one or a combination of the following: uncooked macaroni, rice, or beans; pebbles; bells. Fill the inside of the container with one or more of the ingredients. Decorate your instrument by painting it or covering it with construction paper.

Making Sand Blocks

Find sandpaper, glue, and two blocks of wood. Cover one side of each block with sandpaper, adhering it with a strong glue. Rub the blocks together to the musical tempo.

Making a Tambourine

Get two sturdy paper plates; small bells, shells, buttons, or bottle caps; and string or yarn. Tape, staple, or sew the paper plates together. Punch holes around the outside and tie bells, shells, etc. to plates with string or yarn. Shake to play.

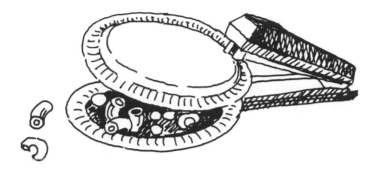

Here are a few suggestions for the use of musical instruments:

- Help your child keep the beat of a favorite song.
- Make two sounds using two different instruments, and ask your child if they are the same or different.
- Ask your child to clap with you while you play an instrument—then let her play while you clap.
- Establish a beat pattern—two fast beats, one slow beat—and ask your child to imitate you.
- Have your child close her eyes as you hide an instrument under a table. Then play it and ask her to name the instrument. Make up a story and use a different instrument to represent each character.

Learning Is Fun

The activities in this chapter will help your child develop, learn, and grow in many ways. Songs that involve pointing to or moving specific body parts will help your child develop body awareness and a sense of self. Learning the words to songs helps to enhance important language skills and concepts, especially when the words relate to specific movements or when the song's theme relates to the child's current experiences.

Music and movement activities that encourage freedom of expression, such as Free Flow Music Fun and Pretend to Be described in this chapter, encourage creativity and spontaneity. Music and rhythm activities that require any sort of movement, from finger plays to action chants and musical games, can help to improve large and small muscle control, strength, and endurance. Musical games and action chants that require movements to take place in a particular order, such as If You're Happy song will help your child learn to follow directions and develop an understanding of sequential action. Some songs and musical activities, such as Name the Instrument, will help your child learn to discriminate sounds, tempos, and melodies. Finally, all the activities in this chapter will improve your child's sense of rhythm and increase her appreciation of music and creative movement.

If you've tried any of these or other music and rhythm games, you know how much they can enhance family fun. Enrich your lives—make music an integral part of your family's daily routine. The radio provides an infinite variety of music, from rock to classical. Borrow records and audio and video tapes from your local library if you don't want to invest in them yourself. Many communities also offer free concerts and dance performances, especially during the summer.

Chapter 7

EXPLORING THE WORLD OF GROUP ACTIVITIES

Remember the excitement of playing musical chairs at your 4th birthday party, or the pride you felt when you hit that first kickball homer at age 7? Sharing group games with family, friends, and peers is one of the most important aspects of a child's heritage of play. Group games provide experiences that promote social and emotional development. Through these games, your child will develop abilities in cooperative play, sharing, and following rules and directions.

Sometimes children with disabilities are left out of group games because their special needs make it difficult to include them. Share the Fun With Everyone games are designed to be enjoyed by all children of any ability level, as well as their parents, other adults, brothers and sisters, and young friends. Remember to keep the children's physical abilities and limitations in mind when setting the rules for the games. If one child doesn't walk, but only crawls, either set the rules to make it a crawling game or pair the child with an older partner who can push the child's wheelchair or stroller or carry him piggyback. Younger children can benefit from the experience of the activity and from being surrounded by other people, even if they do not understand the group process.

Despite the elements of competition that appear in some of these games, everyone should be a winner. The emphasis is not on winning, but rather on physical activity and social interaction. The most important rule is to have fun!

The Rainbow Bunch Shares the Fun With Everyone

The Rainbow Bunch was formed a year ago when Johnny Green's dad talked to his son's special education teacher. He thought a club would be beneficial for Johnny and the rest of the Green family, so he decided to start one himself. Four families decided to join. Assisted by Ginny, a local recreation therapist, the Green, Blue, Gold, Violet, and Red families meet monthly in the school gym to enjoy a variety of activities like those described in *Creative Play Activities for Children With Disabilities*. All the families have become fast friends. "These are all special people," says Mr. Green. "It's wonderful to have found a place where we belong." There may be a similar club or family recreation program near you. Ask your child's teacher for information.

Today the Rainbow Bunch is going to spend their club meeting playing group games. And then, because it is Leslie's birthday, they will have cake and punch. "C'mon," says Ginny, "It's time to get started!"

The Hat Game

These are the ingredients you'll need for this activity:

☆ Hat

☆ Mirror

☆ Formation—circle

Here is the chant you can sing to play the Hat Game:

(NAME) HAS A HAT.

NOW WHAT DO YOU THINK OF THAT?

She takes off the hat and gives it to another player.

Give the hat to your child and tell her to put it on her head. Let her look in a mirror to see herself. Recite the chant. Have her take off the hat and pass it to the next person as she names the person.

Shoe Find Game

You need just your shoes for this activity. The group sits in a circle and everyone takes off his shoes. The group leader puts all shoes in the center of the circle and mixes them up. Each person gets a turn to find his shoes. Another way to play this game is to have the group leader collect one shoe from each person, give one person at a time someone else's shoe, and ask him to find the owner.

The Ball Goes 'Round 'n' 'Round Game

The only ingredient you'll need for this activity is a large ball. When the Rainbow Bunch play this game, they form a circle, sitting close enough to each other to pass the ball around. Johnny Green's dad starts the chant: *The ball goes 'round 'n' 'round* as the ball is passed around the circle. Anyone in the circle can decide to keep the ball. Then the group chants: *Who has the ball?* The person who has the ball responds, *I have the ball*, passing the ball to the next person as the game continues.

The Freeze Game

You can use a tape recorder, radio, record player with instrumental music, or musical instruments to play this game. Members of your group should scatter in a clearly defined space. Put an adult or older child in charge of playing lively music. When the music begins, players move freely around the room in time to the music. When the music stops, tell the group to freeze in their positions for two or three seconds. Begin the music again.

Stress the importance of freedom of movement; encourage everyone to explore and create different ways of moving about the room. If necessary, demonstrate. For example, the group may walk, crawl, hop, skip, gallop, walk backwards or sideways. (See Free Flow Music Fun in chapter 6 [page 158] for ideas on different types of movement.)

Adaptation for the Physically Impaired. For children with mobility impairments, encourage movements with whatever body part the child can move.

Express Train Game

These are the ingredients you'll need for this activity:

☆ A chair or carpet square for each person
☆ Drum or instrumental recording
☆ Obstacle course

Each person in the group begins at an individual station, either sitting in a chair or standing on a carpet square. The stations form a circle or line. One person is selected to be the conductor. The conductor selects someone else to be the first car of the train, and they begin to chug around the room and pick up the other cars at their stations. The train's cars can link together by everyone keeping both hands on the waist or shoulders of the car in front of them. Once all the cars are linked together to form the train, the conductor leads them forwards, backwards, very slow, very fast, and through an obstacle course.

Musical Hoops Game

These are the ingredients you'll need for this activity:

☆ One hula hoop per person
☆ Piano or musical recording

Place the hula hoops flat on the floor to form a circle around the room. When the music starts, the group walks or skips around the hula hoops. When the music stops, each player must jump inside a hoop. Each time the music stops, one hoop is removed, and all the players must work together to ensure that everyone, or at least some part of everyone, shares the remaining hoops. There are only winners in this game!

Balance the Beach Ball Game

You will need one beach ball for each pair of children playing this game. Each child in the group pairs up with another child. The pair tries to hold a beach ball between them without using their hands. The children can explore all the different ways to balance the ball between them—head-to-head, side-to-side, stomach-to-stomach, back-to-back, and so on. They can move around the room while balancing the beach ball, walking sideways or backwards. The whole group can form a beach ball train for a greater challenge and lots of fun.

Beanbag Toss Game

You will need these ingredients for this activity:

☆ Three or more beanbags
☆ Three or more wastebaskets or empty boxes

Divide players into three or more equal lines. Place an empty wastebasket or box about 2 feet from each line. Each player gets at least three consecutive turns to throw the beanbag into the basket. After each player completes the third throw, he collects the beanbags and passes them to the next player. As skill levels improve, move the basket further from the players.

Have children practice the motion of tossing the beanbag underhand. After a few practice swings, have them release the beanbag without aiming. Place the basket close to any child who is having difficulty with throwing a long distance.

Adaptation for the Physically and Visually Impaired. Move the basket closer to the child and attach a large, bright-colored, or shiny object to it. A parent or older child can move the basket to catch the beanbags.

Tunnel Ball Games

These are the ingredients you'll need for these games:

☆ Rubber ball (any size)

☆ Two or more players

Circle Tunnel Ball Game

Players form a circle, sitting on the floor with their legs spread apart. One person stands in the center of the circle with the ball; that person is "it." (A parent can demonstrate first.) "It" rolls the ball towards another player who stops the ball with hands only and rolls the ball back to "it." If the ball rolls outside of the circle, "it" in the center of the circle retrieves it. Allow different players, both children and parents, to be "it."

Center Ball Game

Six or more players stand in a circle with their legs spread apart, their feet touching their neighbors'. Bending at the waist, players roll the ball back and forth on the floor. The players attempt to keep the ball in the circle using their hands and feet as guides.

Adaptation.   This ball game is designed to help small children learn how to handle a ball by practicing rolling and catching. Parents may want to divide the circle into smaller circles to give children more opportunities to handle the ball. Use different-sized balls.

Simple Circle Games

You will need six or more players, and a peanut in a shell, pebble, or button to play the next seven games. See individual activities for additional ingredients.

Duck-Duck-Goose Game

The group leader helps players sit in a circle. Select one player to be "it" and to stand outside the circle. "It" runs around the circle, touches one child after another on the head and says, "duck, duck," etc., until he touches a player of his choice, at which time he says, "goose." The child designated "goose" gets up and chases "it" who must run around the circle back to where "goose" was sitting. If "goose" tags "it" before "it" is seated, then he continues to be "it." If "it" sits down without being tagged, "goose" becomes "it" and the game continues.

Monkey and the Peanut Game

Same procedure as Duck-Duck-Goose. One player is designated as the "monkey." He drops a peanut in one player's lap instead of tagging him.

Raindrop Game

Same procedure as Duck-Duck-Goose. One player is designated as the "rainmaker." He carries a raindrop (a pebble or button) around the circle and drops it into the hand of one of the other players.

Cut the Pie Game

The group forms a circle and holds hands. One child is selected to be "it" and stands in the center. "It" raises his hands over his head and brings his hands down over the joined hands of two circle players to cut the pie. The two children run in opposite directions around the outside of the circle. The first one back into place is the new "it" and the game continues.

Round and Round It Goes Game

You'll need three or four different objects, and recorded music. The group sits in a circle on the floor. The objects are distributed around the circle. When the music starts, the group passes around the objects in the same direction. When the music stops, all players holding an object must go sit in the center. With a small group, use only one object.

Cat and Dog Game

You'll need two stuffed animals, one cat and one dog. The group sits in a circle on the floor. The dog is passed around the circle, then the cat is passed in the same direction. When the cat catches the dog, the game is over.

Pass the Block Game

You'll need one hand-size block or musical instrument bells. The group forms a circle, standing or sitting close together, and "it" stands in the middle of the circle. "It" closes his eyes for a few seconds as the game starts. The block is passed from one person to another behind everyone's backs. When "it" thinks he knows where the block is, he shouts "stop," makes his guess, then opens his eyes. If "it" is correct, he changes places with the person holding the block who then becomes the new "it." If "it" is incorrect, he is given two more guesses before being replaced by another child from the group. Bells can be used instead of the block, which will help to give extra clues.

Red Light, Green Light Game

You'll need a hand made red light and green light (place red and green cellophane over flashlights) to play this game. One child is selected to be the leader, and an adult stands next to him as the leader's helper. The rest of the group stands about 20 feet in front of the leader. The leader turns his back to the group and says, "Green light, GO!" as the adult holds up the green light. The group advances towards the leader. The leader says, "Red light, STOP!" The adult holds up the red light, and all the children must stop. If any child is moving after the leader says "STOP," that child must go back to the starting line. The first child to get to the leader becomes the new leader. The adult may need to assist the leader. You may also use red and green construction paper signs for this game.

Leapfrog Game

Play this game with four or more players. Each player is positioned on hands and knees on the floor, one in front of another, facing the same direction with no space between them. The line of frogs begins at one side of a fairly large room and must get to the other side. The player at the end of the line must leap over all the other frogs by walking or gently hopping over them until he reaches the front of the line. Then the new frog at the end of the line does the same thing. The game continues until everyone gets to the other side of the room or the designated finish line. This game can also be played with two teams.

The Fishing Game

These are the ingredients you'll need for this game:

☆ Fish of different colors and sizes cut out of construction paper

☆ Lightweight magnets, string, and rulers to make fishing rods

☆ Paper clips to attach to nose of each fish

Players sit in a circle on chairs. Scatter fish in the center. Make a fishing rod by tying the magnet to the ruler with a length of string. The magnet will attach itself to the paper clip on the fish. Count the number of fish caught. Tell players to catch a big fish and then a little fish. Tell them to look for a certain color fish and catch it.

Adaptation for Children with Visual Perception Problems.   To assist a child with focusing and visual scanning difficulties, place only one to four fish in a designated area, such as on a carpet square or piece of cardboard. Depending on the child's physical ability, he may need assistance and guidance to manipulate the fishing rod.

Adaptation for the Visually Impaired.   Use aluminum foil or other bright, shiny paper to make fish.

Family Photo Posters Guessing Game

These are the ingredients you'll need for this activity:

- ☆ Large sheet of posterboard
- ☆ Two photos of each family member, including grandparents—one recent photo, one old photo
- ☆ Liquid white glue

Glue pictures onto posterboard at random. Players take turns guessing which two photos are the same person, trying to match up each recent photo with an old one.

Loop De Loo Game

Play this game with two or more players. Use a musical accompaniment. Try using a drum, bongo, or homemade instrument. This game is played with a chant.

Verse 1: I PUT MY RIGHT HAND IN.
I PUT MY RIGHT HAND OUT.
I GIVE MY HAND A SHAKE, SHAKE, SHAKE,
AND TURN MYSELF ABOUT.
Verse 2: I PUT MY LEFT HAND IN, ETC.
Verse 3: I PUT BOTH HANDS IN, ETC.
Verse 4: I PUT MY RIGHT FOOT IN, ETC.
Verse 5: I PUT MY LEFT FOOT IN, ETC.
Verse 6: I PUT MY ELBOWS IN, ETC.
Verse 7: I PUT MY SHOULDERS IN, ETC.
Verse 8: I PUT MY HEAD IN, ETC.
Verse 9: I PUT MY WHOLE SELF IN, ETC.
   Repeat this chorus after each verse:
HERE WE GO LOOP DE LOO,
HERE WE GO LOOP DE LIE,
HERE WE GO LOOP DE LOO,
ALL ON A SATURDAY NIGHT.

Players form a circle holding hands. Players move around the circle in a walking, skipping, or sliding motion, singing the chorus. With each verse the players stop, face the center, and drop hands. Players complete action as verse indicates. Continue with chorus and verses.

Adaptation for the Physically Impaired.   If a child has difficulty moving around the circle, he can perform the walking, skipping, or sliding movements while standing in place. A child in a wheelchair can be pushed or can push himself. For children who cannot distinguish right or left, simply say "hands," "feet," etc. Another alternative is to tie a piece of colored yarn to the child's wrist and use the color to identify right or left.

Lassie Game

These games are played with two or more players. This is the song that accompanies the activities:

DID YOU EVER SEE A LASSIE, A LASSIE, A LASSIE?
DID YOU EVER SEE A LASSIE GO THIS WAY AND THAT?
GO THIS WAY AND THAT WAY, GO THIS WAY AND THAT WAY,
DID YOU EVER SEE A LASSIE GO THIS WAY AND THAT?

Lassie Circle Game

Players join hands and form a circle. "Lassie" stands in center of the circle. Players move around the circle while chanting. Lassie chooses and performs an action. At the words "this way and that," players stop moving around the circle and imitate Lassie's action until the song is over. At the end of the song, Lassie picks a new Lassie. The game continues until all players have had a turn.

Imagination Circle Game

Instead of being the "Lassie," the child in the center chooses what he wants to be: a farmer (pretending to feed chickens), an airplane (flying about the circle with arms outstretched), a tree (swaying body gently back and forth), a duck (walking and making duck sounds), or an elephant (putting hands together, pretending they are the elephant's trunk). For children who have trouble choosing what to be or what action to perform, the parent can suggest an action or a character with which the child is familiar.

Charlie Over the Water Game

This game is played with four or more players. Players join hands and form a circle. One player stands in the center of the circle as "Charlie." As the circle moves to the right or left, Charlie sings the following rhyme.

CHARLIE OVER THE WATER,
CHARLIE OVER THE SEA,
CHARLIE CATCH A BLACKBIRD,
BUT CAN'T CATCH ME.

When Charlie completes the rhyme, players must stoop down before Charlie tags them. Any player who has not stooped down and is tagged by Charlie becomes the new Charlie. The old Charlie joins the circle. Have Charlie approach players in a walking fashion as opposed to running. Try using various positions to stump Charlie— sitting down, raising arms, touching shoulders. Game ends when all players have had a chance to be Charlie.

Adaptation for the Physically Impaired.   When playing with children unable to move around the circle, have players stay in one spot and lift their feet one at a time. Any player who can't stoop down can try bending at the waist. Children who are not mobile from the waist down can touch their heads.

Animal Farm Game

You'll need one hula hoop per pair of children to play this game. Place hula hoops on the floor around an open room. An adult leader whispers into each person's ear the name of an animal and the sound it makes, giving the same animal to two different people. After everyone has been told their animal and sound, the leader says, "Find your partner." Each person makes the sound of his animal until he finds his partner—the same animal. The only means of communication allowed is the animal sound. When the animal partners find one another, they get into a hula hoop together, hold it around their waists, and walk around the room. The leader then calls out for two different groups of animals to find each other, such as, "Horses find cows," "Pigs find sheep," and "Ducks find cats." Each hula hoop pair of animals must find the other designated pair of animals by listening for and identifying their sounds. When the two pairs find each other, they stack their hoops together around themselves so that there are now four players inside two hoops. Follow this activity with a quiet game.

Surprise Jar Game

These are the ingredients you'll need for this game:

☆ Pictures with specific actions to imitate
☆ Jar or box that opens for players to reach into

Place action pictures in the jar. A parent or older child demonstrates by making the first selection and performing the action. Action pictures can include a lively, wiggly worm; an elephant (walk with hands clasped together, bending over at waist, swinging arms as the elephant's trunk); a tree blowing in the wind; a dancer. Other players guess what the child in the center is acting out. Some children may need assistance performing their actions. Try to make tasks fun and appropriate to the abilities of the children involved. Encourage all children to be themselves and use their imaginations.

Fashion Parade Games

For these games you'll need dress-up clothes, including hats, lipstick, ribbons, costume jewelry, sunglasses, and other accessories. You may want to take pictures. An instant camera is the most fun.

Fashion Parade Game

The group leader divides everyone into groups of four and gives each group dress-up clothes and accessories. Each group selects one person to decorate and dress up according to a theme of their choice. Possible themes could be a circus master, a king or queen, a Christmas tree, an Indian rain dancer, a famous movie or T.V. star, or a cartoon character. Each group gets a turn to parade their decorated person as a commentator from the group explains the creation. Capture the model with an instant photo.

Screen Test Game

Each actor dresses up according to a "show-biz" theme of his choice and acts out a very short skit. The rest of the group tries to guess who or what the actor is, and a designated camera person takes a picture of the action.

Name Game

You'll need a ball and four to six players in each group to play this game. One child is selected to be "it." The rest of the group forms a semicircle approximately 15 feet in front of "it." "It" rolls the ball toward the group and calls out one player's name. That player runs out of the group and catches the ball. After he catches the ball, he rolls it back to "it." The game continues until "it" has called all the children's names. Each child should be given an opportunity to be "it."

Parachute Games

To play these games, you'll need a parachute and a large group.

The Cloud Game

One child sits in the center of the parachute; the rest of the group is evenly spaced around it. Each person takes hold with both hands onto the edge of the parachute and shakes it up and down quickly. The chute will surround the child in the center with billows of air, making him feel like he is in the clouds. Each child gets a turn in the center.

Trade Places Game

The group evenly spaces itself around the parachute, and each person takes hold with both hands onto the edge of the parachute. An adult leader calls out, "one, two, three, UP," and the group lifts the parachute together. On the signal "DOWN," the group pulls the parachute down towards the ground. Practice "up" and "down" in rhythm until the group is able to work the parachute together in an even up-and-down motion. Once the group has the hang of this, the leader waits until the parachute is going up, then calls the names of two children. The children must run under the parachute and trade places before the parachute falls to the ground. At the end of the game, once each child has had a turn, all the children step under the parachute and let it fall on top of them.

The Mushroom Game

After the group has made the parachute go up and down several times, get ready to go under it as it is coming down. Everyone quickly takes the edges they are holding under their bottoms and sits down. This creates a puff of air that holds the parachute up as the group is sitting under it. This one may take some practice!

Balloon Games

These are the ingredients you'll need for these activities:

☆ Several inflated balloons or medium-sized beach balls

☆ A volleyball net or one long piece of rope, approximately 10 feet in length

☆ Balloons for each player

☆ 2-foot lengths of string

Here are some balloon games your group can play

Balloon Volleyball

Select two players to hold the rope taut as the volleyball net. Divide players into two equal teams. Place one team on each side of the net. Players take turns hitting a balloon back and forth. Play begins as one team serves the balloon over the net. When one team lets the balloon hit the floor, a point is scored, and the opposite team then serves. At the end of the designated time period, the team with the most points wins.

Adaptation for the Physically Impaired.   Lower the entire volleyball net, or lay a rope on the floor. Use a beach ball or other lightweight ball instead of a balloon.

Bop-Pop Game

Tie a piece of string about 2 feet long to each balloon and tie one to each player's ankle. Players scatter about the room and try to pop each other's balloons by stepping on them. The object of this game is to keep your balloon from being popped!

SAFETY NOTE

Bop-Pop may not be appropriate for children who become frightened by the noise, especially visually impaired children. Any games using balloons should be closely supervised to ensure that children do not mouth or swallow balloons.

Tag Games

These variations on tag need only three or more players to be enjoyable.

Boundary Tag

This is the simplest of all tag games. Any number of children, friends, and family members can play. One player is selected to be "it" while the rest of the group spreads out within a clearly marked area about the size of a basketball court. "It" chases the players until someone is tagged. The person tagged then becomes the new "it" and the game goes on. If a player runs out of the boundary lines, he becomes "it."

Chain Tag

This game requires at least 8 to 10 people to work best. Play in an area that has clearly marked boundaries. The player who is "it" chases everyone until he catches one person. The person who is tagged joins hands with "it," and both try to tag another player. Each player who is tagged joins the chain. If the chain breaks, no one can be tagged until all join hands again. Tagged players always join the end of the chain line away from the original "it."

Adaptation for the Physically Impaired.   Have an adult, brother, or sister push the child's wheelchair, or let the child wheel him to play Boundary Tag.

Relay Games

These are the ingredients you'll need for this set of activities:

☆ Two or more players per team

☆ Three milk cartons

☆ Two lines, 15 feet apart, made with masking tape, designating start and finish. (Adjust the distance between the tape marks depending on children's ages and abilities.)

☆ Inner tube, tire, or hula hoop

☆ Chalk, tape, paint, rope, balloons, soap bubbles

The group leader divides the families into two or more equally numbered teams. Teams are placed parallel to each other with no more than five to eight people per team.

Basic Relay

The group leader cues the team by saying, "Ready, set, go!" Each player performs a specific movement to get to the tape mark and back again. These movements may include walking, hopping, skipping, or sliding. The game ends when all players are in their original positions.

Up 'n' Down Relay

Use one inner tube, tire, or hula hoop for each team, and place three milk cartons in each. One player runs up to the hoop and knocks down the cartons, then the next player runs up and sets them up again. Continue until everyone has had a turn.

In 'n' Out Relay

Use one inner tube, tire, or hula hoop for each team, and place three milk cartons in each. One player puts the cartons outside the tire and the next places them inside. Repeat until everyone has had a turn.

Line Relay

Using tape, paint, chalk, or rope, make specific patterns (straight or curved) on the floor. Each team walks, hops, crawls, or skips down the line. To make it more interesting, have players walk backwards, forwards, and on tiptoes, or take giant or little steps.

Balloon Relay

On hands and knees, each team member must blow the balloon a designated distance (not too far from the starting line), pick the balloon up, and walk back to the starting line. The player then hands the balloon to the next in line. You may want to pair adults or older children with younger or disabled children. HINT: Blow the balloon and crawl behind it, keeping your face close to the ground and the bottom part of the balloon.

Bubble Blow Relay

You need one jar of bubbles and wand per two-person team. This game may be most successful if an older child or adult is paired with a younger or disabled child. Form two lines of competition. One partner holds the jar of bubbles and the wand while the other blows bubbles as both walk swiftly toward the finish line. When players reach the tape mark, they reverse roles and run back to the starting line.

Adaptation for the Physically Impaired.   A child in a wheelchair can wheel himself down the relay line. Or pair the child with another team member who will push the child's wheelchair.

Getting Together

Like the "Rainbow Bunch" and thousands of other families around the world who are members of similar clubs and support groups, you and a small group of other families can meet together once or twice a month to enjoy the kinds of activities described in *Creative Play Activities for Children With Disabilities*. The disabled child and his mother and father, brothers and sisters, and even extended family members and friends can enjoy the friendship, support, and learning that comes from sharing the joy of play. Ask you child's teacher if there is an activity club for you and your family and friends in your community. If not, you can start a club of your own. A teacher, social worker, therapist, or other experienced group leader can help run the club. Why don't you and your family join the fun?

ASSOCIATIONS AND AGENCIES RESOURCE LIST

Organizations Serving Persons With Disabilities and Their Families

Alexander Graham Bell Association for the Deaf, Inc.
3417 Volta Place, NW
Washington, DC 20007
(202)337-5220 (Voice/TDD)

Promotes the effective use of amplified residual hearing and speech-reading skills for children with hearing impairments.

American Association for Deaf Children
814 Thayer Avenue
Silver Spring, MD 20910
(310)585-5400

A clearinghouse for family members of persons who are deaf to exchange information. Provides general information about deafness and raising children with hearing impairments.

American Council of the Blind

1010 Vermont Avenue, NW, Suite 1106
Washington, DC 20005
(800)424-8666

Advocates appropriate legislation for the blind and other handicapped persons. Has general information on blindness which is useful to parents. ACB Parents, a network of blind parents and parents with blind children, produces a newsletter and other services.

American Foundation of the Blind

15 West 16th Street
New York, NY 10011
(212)620-2000

Assists persons who are blind and visually impaired in acquiring improved rehabilitation services and educational and employment opportunities, and aids them in their daily living activities.

American Speech-Language-Hearing Association (ASHA)

10801 Rockville Pike
Rockville, MD 20852
(301)897-8682 (Voice/TDD)

A membership organization of individuals with speech, hearing, and language disorders; their families; and interested professionals. Primarily concerned with advocating the rights of the communicatively impaired and with public information activities.

Association of Birth Defect Children

3201 East Crystal Lake Avenue
Orlando, FL 32806
(305)898-5342

Provides information and support to families of children with birth defects of a nongenetic nature, caused by parents' exposure to drugs, chemicals, radiation, and other environmental agents.

Association for the Care of Children's Health (ACCH)

3615 Wisconsin Avenue, NW
Washington, DC 20016
(202)244-1801

Promotes the health and well-being of children in health care settings and the care of chronically ill and disabled children and their families. Publishes a quarterly journal and a bimonthly newsletter as well as bibliographies.

Association for Children and Adults with Learning Disabilities (ACLD)
4156 Library Road
Pittsburgh, PA 15234
(412)341-1515

Provides general information about learning disabilities as well as advocacy for educational and rehabilitative legislation.

The Association for Persons with Severe Handicaps (TASH)
7010 Roosevelt Way, NE
Seattle, WA 98115
(206)523-8446

Advocates the need for quality education and services for persons with severe handicaps. Membership includes families, educators, lawyers, medical personnel, therapists, psychologists, and social workers. A parent-to-parent network links parents of children with severe handicaps who are involved in local parent-support and advocacy groups.

Association for Retarded Citizens of the United States (ARC)
National Headquarters
2501 Avenue J
Arlington, TX 76011
(817)640-0204

Works to prevent mental retardation, find its cures, and assist mentally retarded persons and their families. ARC works on national, state, and local levels to communicate and interpret the needs of the mentally retarded to the public and to government agencies.

The Candlelighters Foundation
2025 Eye Street, NW
Suite 1011
Washington, DC 20006
(202)659-5136

An international organization of groups of parents who have or have had children with cancer. Distributes bibliographies on childhood cancer, materials for parents, and books about cancer and dying for children. Sponsors conferences, publishes a quarterly newsletter and a newsletter for teens, and serves as a clearinghouse on state and federal programs.

Clearinghouse on the Handicapped
Office of Special Education and Rehabilitative Services
Room 3132 Switzer Building
Washington, DC 20202
(202)732-1245

A federal resource information office designed to answer questions regarding legislation, publications, or programs affecting people with disabilities. Provides resource guides on important issues related to disability. Also publishes a Directory of National Information Sources on Handicapped Conditions and Related Services and "OSERS in Print."

Compassionate Friends, Inc.
P.O. Box 3696
Oak Brook, IL 60522
(312)990-0010

A nationwide support group for bereaved parents. Chapters provide opportunities to share ideas and support related to coping with the death of a child. Publications include pamphlets, booklist, and a national quarterly newsletter.

Cornelia de Lange Syndrome Foundation
60 Dryer Avenue
Collinsville, CT 06022
(203)693-0159

Supports parents and children affected by Cornelia de Lange Syndrome (CdLS), increases public awareness of CdLS, and supports research for CdLS. A directory of parents and interested persons, a pamphlet, and the bimonthly newsletter, Reaching Out, *are available.*

Council for Exceptional Children (CEC)
Information Services
1920 Association Drive
Reston, VA 22091
(703)620-3660

Works to advance the education of exceptional children and youths, both disabled and gifted. CEC Information Services is an information broker for teachers, administrators, students, families, and others. Produces numerous publications on special education, awareness of disabled people, child abuse, recreation, parent-professional cooperation, career and vocational education, severely disabled children, and public policy. Bibliographies on topics of current interest and nonprint media also available.

Cystic Fibrosis Foundation
6931 Arlington Road
Bethesda, MD 20814
(301)951-4422

Works for the prevention, control, and effective treatment of cystic fibrosis.

Down's Syndrome Congress
Central Office
1800 Dempster Street
Park Ridge, Il 60068
(312)226-0416
(800)446-3835

Members in chapters throughout the country share experiences with other parents and professionals working for the public awareness and civil rights of this population. An annual convention, a 10-issue newsletter, and a quarterly publication keep the membership informed of new medical, legislative, and educational developments.

Epilepsy Foundation of America
4351 Garden City Drive, Suite 406
Landover, MD 20785
(301)459-3700

Advocates and provides a wide variety of services and programs for the person with epilepsy. Publishes pamphlets, reprints, books, cassettes, slides, films, a directory of clinics, and a monthly newsletter. Also has medical resource data base available on an individual basis upon request.

Human Growth Foundation
4930 West 77th Street
Minneapolis, MN 55435
(612)831-2780

A membership organization of parents of children with severe physical growth problems and professionals specializing in the field of growth retardation.

International Institute for the Visually Impaired, 0-7, Inc.
1975 Rutgers Circle
East Lansing, MI 48823

A clearinghouse of information for teachers, parents, and others concerned with the early development and education of visually handicapped preschool children and with the education of their families.

Juvenile Diabetes Foundation International
432 Park Avenue South
New York, NY 10016
(212)889-7575

Supports and funds research on the treatment and cure of diabetes—mainly juvenile diabetes (also called insulin-dependent diabetes), which has its onset anywhere from infancy to the late 30s. The organization publishes free pamphlets and fact sheets about diabetes and insulin for the layperson.

Know Problems of Hydrocephalus
c/o Mazzetti
Route 1, River Road, Box 210A
Joliet, IL 60436

A support group and organization for people with hydro-cephalus and their family members.

Little People of America
Box 633
San Bruno, CA 94066
(415)589-0695

A nationwide organization for dwarfs providing fellowship, an interchange of ideas, moral support, and solutions to the problems unique to the little person. A special membership division provides information exchange and group support to parents of dwarfed children and their siblings. Publications include a newsletter and printed materials on equipment and aids, clothing, and social and vocational adjustment.

Mental Health Association
1800 North Kent Street
Arlington, VA 22209
(703)528-6405

Offers referral services to parents of emotionally disturbed children. Some affiliates provide parent support services.

Muscular Dystrophy Association (MDA)
810 Seventh Avenue
New York, NY 10019
(212)586-0808

Supports research into neuromuscular disorders. Provides medical care and other direct services free to persons who have muscular dystrophy. Local chapters sponsor recreational activities (e.g., summer camps, picnics, and outings) and organize self-help groups for persons with muscular dystrophy and their families.

National Alliance for the Mentally Ill (NAMI)
1901 North Fort Meyer Drive, Suite 500
Arlington, VA 22209
(703)524-7600

Distributes literature on emotional and behavioral problems. State affiliates provide support services.

National Association for the Deaf-Blind
2703 Forest Oak Circle
Norman, OK 73071

Furthers educational, rehabilitation, and employment opportunities fors persons who are deaf-blind.

National Association for Sickle-Cell Disease
3460 Wilshire Boulevard
Suite 1012
Los Angeles, CA 90010

Provides an extensive public and professional education program about sickle-cell disease, its variants, and sickle-cell trait. A Home Study Kit for Families includes printed materials, cassettes, games, and other learning devices to help parents and other family members cope with the problems they may have.

National Association for the Visually Handicapped
22 West 21st Street
New York, NY 10010
(212)889-3141

*Provides information, referral, and direct services for per-
sons with visual handicaps and their families.*

National Down Syndrome Society
141 Fifth Avenue
New York, NY 10018
(212)460-9330
(800)221-402

*Promotes research into and public awareness and education
regarding Down Syndrome. Provides a toll-free hotline, free
printed information packets, a videocassette, and a
directory of all early intervention and parents' support
groups.*

National Easter Seal Society
2023 West Ogden Avenue
Chicago, IL 60612
(312)243-8400
(312)243-8880 (TDD)

*Local chapters provide direct rehabilitation services to per-
sons with disabilities. Publishes a variety of books, pamphlets, and reprints for professionals, families, and persons
with disabilities.*

National Head Injury Foundation
333 Turnpike Road
Southboro, MA 01772
(617)485-9950

*Assists head-injured persons and their families in seeking
out needed resources and services. Facilitates the formation
of family support groups in many locations throughout the
country.*

**National Information Center for Handicapped Children
and Youth**
1555 Wilson Boulevard, Suite 700
Rosslyn, VA 22209
(703)522-0870

A federally sponsored program that collects and shares information and ideas that are helpful to handicapped children and youth and the people who care for and about them. The center also answers questions, links people with others who share common concerns, sponsors workshops, and publishes newsletters.

The National Society for Children and Adults with Autism
1234 Massachusetts Avenue, N.W.
Suite 1017
Washington, DC 20005-4599
(202)783-0125

A membership organization of parents, siblings, professionals, and interested people who work for legislation, education, and research for the benefit of all children with severe disorders of communication and behavior. Offers a national sibling organization, SHARE. Publishes a bimonthly newsletter and an annual Proceedings of Society National Conferences.

National Tuberous Sclerosis Association, Inc.
P.O. Box 159
Laguna Beach, CA 92652

A membership organization of parents and concerned physicians of patients with this genetic disorder. Members offer counseling, referral, and support services to other families of persons with tuberous sclerosis.

The Orton Dyslexia Society
724 York Road
Baltimore, MD 21204
(301)296-0232

An international membership organization for professionals and parents of dyslexic children. Disseminates information related to dyslexia and refers persons with dyslexia and parents of children with dyslexia to available resources for diagnosis, remediation, and tutoring.

Osteogenesis Imperfecta Foundation
P.O. Box 428
Van Wert, OH 45891
(419)238-9678

A membership organization of parents of children with this genetic defect. Provides information about medical facilities and services, care and management techniques, and equipment.

Parent Network
1301 E. 38th Street
Indianapolis, IN 46205

A national coalition of individuals and organizations serving persons with special needs.

Prader-Willi Syndrome Association
3515 Malibu Drive
Edina, MN 55436
(612)933-0113

Membership organization of parents and professionals who share knowledge and experience about the Prader-Willi syndrome and how to manage it.

Sibling Information Network
Attention: Lisa Rappanikou
991 Main Street, Suite 3A
East Hartford, CT 06108

Serves as a bridge for sharing ideas, programs, research, or needs regarding siblings and families of persons with disabilities. Publishes the Sibling Information Network Newsletter quarterly.

Siblings for Significant Change
Room 808
823 United Nations Plaza
New York, NY 10017

Unites siblings of handicapped individuals for advocacy, to disseminate information, to offer conferences and workshops for and about siblings and families of handicapped people, and to promote greater public awareness of the needs of the disabled and their families.

SIBS
123 Golden Lane
London, EC1Y ORT
England, United Kingdom

*A support and information service offered by the National
Society for Mentally Handicapped Children and Adults
(MENCAP). Publishes a periodic newsletter for members.*

Spina Bifida Association of America
1700 Rockville Pike
Rockville, MD 20852
(301)770-7222
(800)621-3141

*An outgrowth of the National Easter Seal Society, providing
a resource for local chapters throughout the United States.
Provides information and offers referrals for parents, adults
with spina bifida, and medical professionals.*

United Cerebral Palsy Association (UCPA)
66 East 34th Street
New York, NY 10016
(212)481-6300

*Promotes prevention of cerebral palsy and provides
community-based services for those affected by cerebral
palsy and their families.*

Magazines and Newsletters

The following magazines and newsletters address everyday concerns and topics from educational to medical.

Crisscross
Parentele
1301 E. 38th Street
Indianapolis, IN 46205

*Parentele is a national coalition created and run by volun-
teers. Parents are linked through a national communication
system divided into ten regions. Parentele's quarterly newsletter is full of interesting news and useful resources from
the various regions and provides a reader exchange service.*

The Exceptional Parent Magazine
The Exceptional Parent
605 Commonwealth Avenue
Boston, MA 02215
(617)536-8961

Provides straightforward, practical information to siblings, parents, and others involved with children and young adults with disabilities.

Pediatrics for Parents
Pediatrics for Parents, Inc.
171 Mount Hope Avenue
Bangor, ME 04401

A monthly newsletter for parents, focusing on health topics and parenting tips.

Special Parent, Special Child
Special Parent, Special Child
Lindell Press, Inc.
P.O. Box 462
South Salem, NY 10590

Focuses on parenting and highlights various topics and their relationship to parenting a disabled child.

Books on Play

The Gift of Play: And Why Young Children Cannot Thrive Without It
Walker & Company
720 Fifth Avenue
New York, NY 10019

by Maria W. Piers and Genevieve Millet Landau; 1980

Explores the significance of play for children in every facet of their growth and development and how play helps the disabled child. The book includes an excellent section on the effect of television on children's play behavior.

Kids and Play
Ballantine Books
201 E. 50th Street
New York, NY 10022

by Joanne F. Oppenheim; 1984

Prepared by the Bank Street College of Education, the book is a practical guide explaining what, how, and, most important, why play is basic to the child's total development.

Let Me Play
Souvenir Press/(Educational & Academic), Ltd.
43 Great Russell Street
London, England WC1B PA/or
Methuen Publications
Agincourt, Ontario, Canada

by Dorothy M. Jeffree, Roy McConkey, and Simon Hewson;
1977

> *Written primarily for parents, the emphasis of the book is
> on encouraging the child's play and the link between play
> and development. The book also focuses on practical sug-
> gestions for setting the play environment for disabled
> children.*

**Partners in Play: A Step-By-Step Guide to Imaginative
Play in Children**
Harper & Row Publishers
10 E. 53rd Street
New York, NY 10022

by Jermone L. Singer; 1977

> *A practical book that explains the basic principles of
> fantasy play. Explains, in a step-by-step format, explicit
> games that develop and encourage make-believe play.*

Books on Play Activities and Games for the Infant, Toddler, and Preschool Child

***Baby Learning Through Baby Play
The Baby Exercise Book**
Random House
400 Hahn Road
Westminister, MD 21157

by Janine Levy; 1974

> *Exercises to benefit the infant's physical development,
> emotional stability, and relationships with parents during
> the first 15 months are described and illustrated. The exer-
> cises are based on movements that infants normally make.
> Complete photographic demonstrations are easy to follow.*

---

*NOTE. The resources marked with an asterisk (*) can be
ordered from Toys 'N' Things Press, 906 North Dale Street, St.
Paul, MN 55103, (612) 488-7284.

The Playgroup Handbook
St. Martin's Press, Inc.
175 Fifth Avenue
New York, NY 10010

by Laura Broad and Nancy T. Butterworth; 1974
by Ira J. Gordon; 1970

This guide to games for babies is a practical and simple way to stimulate children under two. The games bring pleasure, security, and physical and intellectual growth to babies.

Child Learning Through Child Play
St. Martin's Press, Inc.
175 Fifth Avenue
New York, NY 10010

by Ira J. Gordon; 1972

Learning activities for 2- and 3-year-olds are presented in a simply written format with many illustrations.

Constructive Play
Addison-Wesley
Reading, MA 01867

by George Forman and Fleet Hill

Over 100 intriguing games have been developed from Piaget's principles of child development. They are all open-ended activities that allow children to design their own rules and play at their own pace. Activities include Drawing Drive, Blip School, Crazy Brushes, Water Pencil, and Speed Bumps.

Everybody Wins
Walker & Company
720 Fifth Avenue
New York, NY 10019

by Jeff Sobel; 1982

This collection contains a wealth of non-competitive games for use with children ages 3-10. The 393 games require very little equipment and are easily adaptable to a variety of situations. There are word games, games of imagination, passive games, and active games—all with the common thread of sharing and cooperation.

Learning Games For Infants and Toddlers
New Readers
Division of Laubach Literacy International
Box 131
Syracuse, NY 13210

by Ronald Lally and Ira J. Gordon; 1977

A playtime handbook for parents and care givers who are low-level readers. Games for ages 2 months to 2 years are listed according to age and learning area and require only ordinary household items and the infant's own toys.

Learning Games For The First Three Years
Berkley Publishing Corporation
Affiliate of G.P. Putnam's Sons
200 Madison Avenue
New York, NY 10016

by Joseph Sparling; 1984

These 100 games are arranged to reflect typical patterns of child development. They are organized by 6-month age spans, each prefaced with a useful checklist on which to note the child's own progress.

*Learning Games For The Threes And Fours
Walker & Company
720 Fifth Avenue
New York, NY 10019

by Joseph Sparling & Isabelle Lewis; 1984

This sequel to the highly successful Learning Games For the First Three Years *shows parents and teachers how to give preschoolers an excellent head start in developing key skills for school success. Grouped into 6-month age spans, 100 imaginative, fun games promote independence, sharing, cooperation, language development, reasoning skills, coordination, creativity, and self-confidence.*

*The Playgroup Handbook

St. Martin's Press
175 Fifth Avenue
New York, NY 10010

by Laura Broad and Nancy T. Butterworth; 1974

You need never run out of exciting and fun ideas for active preschoolers. While addressed to parents who are organizing play groups, the variety of seasonal and nonseasonal activities are terrific for anyone working with this age group.

*Playtime Learning Games

Syracuse University Publishing in Continuing Education
Syracuse, NY 13210

by Alice Honig; 1982

No special materials are needed for this easy-to-use handbook of games to help teach thinking skills to children 2 to 5 years of age. Simple instructions explain what you need, what to do, variations, and the purpose of the games.

*The Sourcebook

Wadsworth Publishing Company
Division of Wadsworth, Inc.
10 Davis Drive
Belmont, CA 94002

by George Maxim; 1980

Thousands of ideas are contained in this collection of exciting activities for infants and young children. The infant section includes physical activity, concept games, language growth, and physical care. The preschool section contains delightfully illustrated ideas on self-concept, physical activity, large muscle development, academic skills, creative activities, and cooking. The activities are indexed by skill area.

*You and Your Small Wonder: Book 1 (Birth to 18 Months); You and Your Small Wonder: Book 2 (18-36 Months)

American Guidance Service, Inc.
Publisher's Building
Circle Pines, MN 55014

by Merle B. Karnes; 1982, 1984

The author presents over 150 activities conveniently arranged to fit into a parent's busy schedule: at changing time, at bath time, when doing household chores, when the whole family is gathered around, or when alone with baby. The activities give practice in eleven essential skills, including language development, balance and motion, and social skills.

Books on Arts and Crafts

*Art for the Fun of It
Prentice-Hall, Inc.
P.O. Box 500
Englewood Cliffs, NJ 07632

by Peggy D. Jenkins; 1980

This manual combines an explanation of the principles of art education with descriptions of hundreds of activities in pasting, tearing and cutting, painting, woodworking, stitchery, puppet making, etc.

Arts and Crafts for Special Education
Fearson-Pitnam Publishers, Inc.
6 Davis Drive
Belmont, CA 94002

by Maryan T. Winsor; 1972

This book provides easy-to-follow directions for more than 100 art projects. Activities are organized by months, from September to June, and include complete directions.

*Don't Move the Muffins
Prentice-Hall, Inc.
P.O. Box 500
Englewood Cliffs, NJ 07632

by Beverly J. Bos; 1982

A splendid, practical guide to art for 2-to5-year-olds. Activities include using paper, paint, crayons, felt pens, and chalk. Collages, holiday art, sculpture, and special art activities complete this "hands-on" guide to art for the young child.

Puppet Factory
Incentive Publications, Inc.
3835 Cleghorn Ave.
Nashville, TN 37215

by Imogene Forte; 1984

This book provides a variety of fun and easy-to-make puppets with clear and simple directions. It also includes ideas for a puppet stage production.

Books on Music and Creative Movement

*Danceplay
New American Library
1633 Broadway
New York, NY 10019

by Diane Lynch-Fraser; 1983

This handbook of exercises for ages 18 months to 4 years is designed to enhance the intellectual, emotional, and social growth of children through body movement. The activities are arranged in three levels of difficulty. Above all, these games and exercises are a source of fun and sharing between adult and child.

*Eye Winker, Tom Tinker, Chin Chopper
Doubleday & Company, Inc.
501 Franklin Avenue
Garden City, NY 11530

by Tom Glazer; 1978

A delightful collection of 50 fingerplays and folksongs from one of the country's foremost balladeers. Piano arrangements and guitar chords are included.

*Music for Ones and Twos
Doubleday & Company, Inc.
501 Franklin Avenue
Garden City, NY 11530

by Tom Glazer; 1983

Over 50 traditional and original songs, games, and finger play rhymes are included in this delightful collection that is definitely not just for ones and twos.

Target on Music
Ivybrook Day School [Formerly Christ Church Child Center]
11614 Seven Locks Road
Rockville, MD 20854

by Ruthlee F. Adler in collaboration with Lillian R. Davis; 1982

Developed by a music therapist with 20 years' experience for children with disabilities ranging from autism to hearing impairments to multiple handicaps. Included are over 100 activities to enhance learning through music. The activities cover the use of movement, rhythm, and music in five major areas: motor skills, communication, sensory integration, concept development, and social interaction.

*Your Baby Needs Music
St. Martin's Press
175 Fifth Avenue
New York, NY 10010

by Barbara Cass-Beggs; 1980

With five sections of music for each stage from the newborn baby to the 2-year-old child, this book is designed for parents, family day care providers, and teachers. It includes words and simple music for lullabies, croons, and songs. You don't have to be a musician to provide music for baby.

Resources for Making and Selecting Toys

Able Data
National Rehabilitation Information Center
8455 Colesville Rd. Suite 935
Silver Spring, MD 20910
(301)588-9284

A computerized data base of commercially available rehabilitation aids and equipment. Includes listings of toys, sensory aids, and play and recreation equipment adapted to the needs of disabled persons.

Lekotek Guide to Good Toys
Lekotek
613 Dempster Street
Evanston, IL 60201

by Mary Sinker; 1983

Descriptions of carefully selected commercial toys for dis-
abled children by the Lekotek Organization. The guide has
divided toys into different areas. Also include therapeutic
equipment and books.

The More We Do Together: Adapting the Environment for Children With Disabilities
World Rehabilitation Fund, Inc.
400 East 34th Street
New York, NY 10016

by The Nordic Committee on Disability in cooperation with
World Rehabilitation Fund; 1985

A practical and valuable book of ideas about technical aids
for children with disabilities. It may serve as an introduc-
tion for parents and others who concern themselves with
adapting the environment. An especially good resource for
the parents of a child with a physical disability.

Smart Toys
Harper & Row Publishing, Inc.
10 E. 53rd Street
New York, NY 10022

by Kent G. Burtt and Karen Kalkstein; 1981

Seventy-seven easy-to-make toys to stimulate babies from
birth to 2 years. A lively text describes the successive
phases of development, concentrating on behaviors perti-
nent to the infant's developing intelligence and play with
toys. Patterns for toys include a complete list of materials,
step-by-step instructions, and clear line drawings.

Teachables From Trashables
Toys 'N' Things Press
906 North Dale Street
St. Paul, MN 55103

A practical, step-by-step guide to making toys for infants
through school-age children. Made from recycled household
materials, these inexpensive toys each have illustrated

directions, age guidelines, suggested play activities, and descriptions of the skills children learn while playing with the toy.

Telephone Pioneers of America
22 Cortland Street, 25th floor
New York, NY 10007
(212)393-2784

Local chapters of this voluntary organization of telephone company employees design and provide adapted recreational equipment to organizations, families, and individuals. Equipment includes a beeping baseball, an audio bouncing ball, a "cricket" to attach to bicycles for persons with visual impairments, and a hand operated tricycle and wagon for children with motor impairments of the lower body.

Contact your local telephone company for information on how to find your local chapter of Telephone Pioneers of America.

Toys Guide: Gifts for Special Children
Pam Assistance Center for the Physically Impaired Association of Michigan
601 West Maple Street
Lansing, MI 48906

List of toys for disabled children from preschool through elementary age.

Commercial Sources of Toys and Equipment for Play and Recreation

Able-Child
154 Chambers Street
New York, NY 10007

Toys and equipment adapted to meet the needs of children with disabilities, including specially designed equipment for children with physical disabilities.

Discovery Toys
400 Ellinwood Way, Suite 300
Pleasant Hill, CA 94523
(415)680-8697

Durable, educational, and fun toys for very young children through elementary age. Most of the toys have a wide range of uses, features, and educational values.

Flaghouse
18 West 18th Street
New York, NY 10011
(212)989-9700

Specially designed play and recreation equipment, including large outdoor equipment, for children with disabilities.

Pediatric Projects
P.O. Box 1880
Santa Monica, CA 90406

Toys to help children adjust to a hospital stay, such as miniature hospital equipment, dolls with special medical conditions, etc.

Toys for Special Children
c/o Stephen Kanor, Medical Engineer
Hastings-on-Hudson, NY 10706

A selection of battery operated toys, specially engineered for children with severe motor impairments.

Records

Hap Palmer Records
Educational Activities, Inc.
Attn.: Sales Department
1937 Grand Avenue
Baldwin, NY 11510

The following series of records by Hap Palmer are specially produced for young children. These records use simple directions and music to help the children to explore areas of body awareness, language concepts, creative movement, and imagination.

Learning Basic Skills Through Music, Getting to Know Myself, Feelin' Free, Movin', Easy Does It, Seagulls, Holiday Songs and Rhymes.

*The Baby Record

These bouncing rhymes, finger and toe plays, games, and lullabies are adapted from successful parent-child inter-action classes. Titles include Ride Baby Ride, Baby A Go Go, This Little Pig Goes to Market, Humpty Dumpty, Shakers, Starlight, This Little Pig Had a Rub a Dub Dub, Ring Around the Rosy, Sleep My Babe, and many more! Available in album or cassette.

*Singable Songs for the Very Young

These are truly "Singable Songs" by one of Canada's most popular children's recording artists. Some are traditional, such as Baa Baa Black Sheep, and others are unique and delightful, like Willoughby Wallaby Woo. Also included are Spider on the Floor, Going to the Zoo, Peanut Butter Sandwich, Five Little Pumpkins, The Sharing Song, Brush Your Teeth, Bumping Up and Down, Must Be Santa Claus, and more. Lyrics are included with the album. Please specify album or cassette.

*You'll Sing a Song and I'll Sing a Song

Everybody loves Ella Jenkins, and this is the album children ask for over and over again. Songs include You'll Sing A Song and I'll Sing A Song, Shabot Shalom, Cadima, This Train, Did You Feed My Cow?, Miss Mary Mack, May-Ree Mack, Dulce Dulce, I Saw, Sifting in the Sand, Guide Me, and more. Notes and text included. Album only.

ABOUT THE
AUTHORS

Lisa Rappaport Morris has a master's degree in communication disorders and clinical education from John Hopkins University. She was program coordinator for the Let's Play to Grow program of the Joseph P. Kennedy, Jr. Foundation from 1983 to 1987. Her eight years of experience in hospital and community settings and in early childhood special education provide much of the practical wisdom in *Creative Play Activities for Children With Disabilities.*

Linda Schulz is a consultant to various local and national organizations in the areas of rehabilitation and special education. She was director of the Let's Play to Grow program from 1983 to 1988 and is a former vice president of the National Organization on Disability. Ms. Schulz has a postgraduate Diploma in Special Education Studies from Oxford University and spent ten years researching programs for the disabled in China, Hong Kong, Japan, and the United Kingdom.